Scott Foresman

Reading

Grade 5

Tennessee
Leveled Practice
and Test Link

Scott Foresman

Editorial Offices: Glenview, Illinois • Parsippany, New Jersey • New York, New York
Sales Offices: Parsippany, New Jersey • Duluth, Georgia • Glenview, Illinois
Carrollton, Texas • Ontario, California

Contents

Leveled Practice

© Scott Foresman 5

Test-Taking Strategies and Skills

Improving Written Answers on Tests

Practice Reading and Writing Tests

Tennessee Curriculum Framework

ISBN: 0-328-00629-7

2345678910-V034-07060504030201

© Scott Foresman 5

Notes to the Teacher

This book is designed to provide leveled practice in reading comprehension skills and prepare students to take state tests administered in Tennessee. All of the student pages are reproducible. They include the following: (1) weekly leveled practice to strengthen comprehension skills taught in *Scott Foresman Reading* and practice using the TerraNova test format, (2) exercises that develop test-taking strategies and skills, (3) activities to help students improve written answers on tests, and (4) a TerraNova practice reading and language arts test and a TCAP writing test to prepare students for state tests given in fifth and seventh grades. The book as a whole helps you prepare students to become better test-takers and writers.

How to Use the Leveled Practice Pages

The purpose of the Leveled Practice pages is to give weekly leveled practice in target comprehension skills taught in *Scott Foresman Reading*, while at the same time providing practice in the TerraNova test format.

This book contains three Leveled Practice pages to be used in conjunction with each main selection in *Scott Foresman Reading*. The pages focus on the target comprehension skill of the week, but are written to address varying levels of proficiency—Easy (E), On-Level (OL), and Challenge (C). A code at the bottom of each page tells you the level of the page.

Easy pages provide a short passage—thematically related to the main selection—on which all of the comprehension questions are based. On-Level and Challenge pages have students return to the main selections in the Student Edition to apply the comprehension skills they are learning.

After students have read the main selection and discussed and practiced the target comprehension skill, you can assign the Leveled Practice pages based on students' proficiency level. You can assess students' proficiency levels using their responses to oral comprehension questions and the Comprehension Check questions, as well as their work on the comprehension pages in the Practice Book or Teacher's Resource Book. Leveled Practice pages can be done independently, or you may choose to work through them with students in small groups, in order to give support and assess student progress.

Other ways to use the Leveled Practice pages:

- use the Easy pages for whole-class practice with the comprehension skill and/or test-taking skills

- use the Easy pages after introducing the skill lesson, prior to reading the main selection, to assess students' readiness to read the main selection

- use the On-Level pages as an assessment tool to check students' understanding of the comprehension skills and/or test-taking skills

- use the On-Level pages to check students' need for further practice, reteaching, or more challenging materials

- use the Challenge pages as a substitute for the comprehension pages in the Practice Book or Teacher's Resource Book for students working above grade level

- use any of the pages as preparation for the reading unit test

How to Use the Test Link Pages

Use the Test-Taking Strategies pages in several sittings before you administer the practice reading and writing tests. Use the Improving Written Answers on Tests pages in conjunction with each unit in the *Scott Foresman Reading* Student Edition. Administer the TerraNova practice reading and language arts test shortly before you give the actual test. Administer the TCAP practice writing test toward the end of the school year.

Answer Key
Leveled Practice

© Scott Foresman 5

Page 1
1. C; 2. F; 3. C
4. Answers may vary, but the steps should be presented in chronological order.

Page 2
1. D; 2. H; 3. B; 4. G
5. Answers could suggest that good problem solvers must identify the problem and think about the best way to address it.

Page 3
1. C; 2. J; 3. C
4. Answers will vary but should acknowledge that the Rampanion must be taken out of its bag and unfolded before it is placed on a curb.
5. Comparisons will vary but should be supported with examples from the text.

Page 4
1. B; 2. J; 3. A
4. Answers should be written from Rufus's point of view and should mention that he is fond of his owner and will miss her when she's at school.

Page 5
1. C; 2. F; 3. A; 4. J
5. Answers may vary, but should be well supported.

Page 6
1. B; 2. J; 3. A
4. Answers will depend on the words students choose, but selection should be a reasonable reflection of the text's content.
5. Answers will vary, but they should be relevant to the text.

Page 7
1. B; 2. H; 3. A
4. Answers should include generalization words, and should also be well supported.

Page 8
1. B; 2. F; 3. C; 4. H
5. Answers will vary but may include generalizations about the Naillings's firmness, kindness, and efforts to make Lee feel like a part of the family.

Page 9
1. D; 2. H; 3. B

Page 10
1. A; 2. J; 3. C
4. Answers may vary, but they should give detailed examples. Possible answers: The bases were loaded, one of the fastest runners was on third, and the catcher missed the tag.

Page 11
1. B; 2. J; 3. B; 4. H
5. Answers may vary, but students will most likely conclude that Mr. Henry wants Jason to identify with them and their struggles.

Page 12
1. B; 2. F; 3. C
4. Answers may vary slightly, but students should conclude that Mr. Henry looked and acted younger when he went into a full wind-up to throw an imaginary baseball.
5. Answers will vary depending on which characters the students choose, but all answers should be well supported.

Page 13
1. D; 2. G; 3. B
4. Answers may vary, but they should go beyond facts provided in the article and mention specifics directly related to the students' own lives.

Page 14
1. B; 2. F; 3. B; 4. G
5. Answers may observe that the pictures help the reader visualize the story and the people better and make the account more interesting.

Page 15
1. D; 2. F; 3. D
4. Answers should acknowledge that the author was trying to show how much her mother wanted the house.
5. Answers will vary, but students should cite specific examples of descriptive, sensory language.

Page 16
1. D; 2. H; 3. C
4. Answers will vary, but should include each of the steps in the process.

Page 17
1. C; 2. G; 3. D; 4. H
5. Answers may vary, but should be adequately supported with textual evidence.

Page 18
1. C; 2. G; 3. C
4. Answers may vary slightly. Possible answer: Identify the individuals; enter the water and wait to be approached by the dolphins; study their noises, movements, and behaviors.
5. Answers may vary slightly, but they should include events in chronological order.

Page 19
1. B; 2. F; 3. C
4. Answers will vary, but it could be a good day to fly a kite or roller-skate.

Page 20
1. C; 2. G; 3. D; 4. H
5. Answers may vary, but they should acknowledge that modern technology and groups such as hurricane fliers provide safety information.

Page 21
1. A; 2. J; 3. C
4. Answers may vary. Students should include chronological steps in the process of the birth of a hurricane and may include terms such as "warm air" and "low pressure."
5. Answers may vary, but students should support their answers with examples from the text.

Page 22
1. C; 2. J; 3. D
4. Answers may vary, but should be accurate in distinguishing fact from opinion. Answers should acknowledge that sentences containing the words *best, worst,* and *nicest* express opinions.

Page 23
1. A; 2. J; 3. A; 4. G
5. Sentence one, which contains the word *greatest,* expresses an opinion. Sentence two, which contains *In my opinion* and *all,* expresses an opinion. Sentence three, which can be proven true or false, expresses a fact.

Page 24
1. D; 2. F; 3. B
4. Answers should accurately distinguish between fact and opinion by establishing which statements are provable and which are not.
5. Answers may vary but should include points to support their claim.

Page 25
1. A; 2. H; 3. D
4. Answers may vary, but should have a sufficient explanation of the author's viewpoint.

Page 26
1. C; 2. J; 3. A; 4. G
5. Answers may vary, but students should show an understanding that this new ending, with the children's eagerness to grow up and change the Earth, presents hope for the future.

Page 27
1. C; 2. J; 3. D
4. Answers may vary, but they should be supported with strong examples of the vivid and poetic descriptions that portray the beauty of the area.
5. Answers may vary, but they should include examples from the two texts, indicating an understanding of their viewpoint.

Page 28
1. D; 2. H; 3. D
4. Answers may vary slightly, but should demonstrate an understanding of deduction and logic.

Page 29
1. C; 2. G; 3. D; 4. G
5. Answers may vary, but they should indicate an ability to draw conclusions and/or make generalizations about textual evidence.

Page 30
1. C; 2. J; 3. B
4. Answers will vary, but students will most likely conclude that the salesman and the baker are no longer there and that the jewelry case is either covered up or the glass has been replaced.
5. Answers will vary. Some students will think that his keen powers of observation, his intelligence, and his stubbornness about the tie would make him a good investigator.

Page 31
1. D; 2. H; 3. C
4. Answers may vary, but should be well supported.

Page 32
1. A; 2. H; 3. C; 4. J
5. Answers may vary, but students should conclude that the experience changes his mind about the new school by letting him be part of a team and making him feel needed.

Page 33
1. B; 2. F; 3. C
4. Answers may vary, but students should generally conclude that Mark changes his opinion of the school after experiencing a sense of belonging.
5. Answers should indicate a grasp of inference based on contextual clues.

Page 34
1. A; 2. G; 3. C
4. Answers may vary, but students should conclude that without delays, the train from Barnaby would arrive at 3:55 P.M., as scheduled.

Page 35
1. B; 2. H; 3. C; 4. J
5. Answers may vary slightly, but they should indicate the ability to read maps for information.

Page 36
1. C; 2. H; 3. D
4. Answers may vary, but they should demonstrate an accurate assessment of graphics as sources of information.
5. Answers may vary, but they should indicate an understanding of the purpose of different types of graphics to supply information.

Page 37
1. D; 2. G; 3. C
4. Answers will vary, but should include a main idea (conflict) and a logical sequence of events that led to a solution.

Page 38
1. B; 2. H; 3. D; 4. F
5. Answers may vary, but they should acknowledge that given Lupe's persistent character, she would most likely continue in her goal to be a marble champ, or perhaps pursue some other sport.

Page 39
1. C; 2. J; 3. A
4. Answers may vary, but they should identify the main conflict and explain its resolution.
5. Answers may vary, but they will probably conclude that Lupe would be disappointed but would resolve to try harder and keep practicing.

Page 40
1. B; 2. J; 3. D
4. Students should conclude that bold or heavy type is a reading aid.

Page 41
1. B; 2. G; 3. C; 4. J

5. Answers may vary, but should list events in chronological order from April through the fall.

Page 42
1. A; 2. H; 3. C
4. Students should begin with a description of the beekeeper's hat and work downward. They should mention gloves, which appear in the photo but not in the written description on page 288.
5. Answers may vary slightly, but should conclude that the report should include steps in the correct order.

Page 43
1. A; 2. H; 3. D
4. Students should realize that the first sentence in the article gives the best summary because it states the main idea without giving all the details.

Page 44
1. C; 2. H; 3. D; 4. F
5. Answers may vary, but they should demonstrate an ability to make comparisons across two different texts.

Page 45
1. C; 2. F; 3. B
4. Answers may vary, but they should demonstrate an ability to make comparisons across two texts.
5. Answers will vary, but they should effectively and accurately assess the main points of the story and include imaginative description.

Page 46
1. C; 2. G; 3. A
4. Answers may vary, but they should make direct connections. Possible answer: They were alike because they both had cake and different because one was at home and the other was at a bowling alley.

Page 47
1. D; 2. H; 3. A; 4. F
5. Answers may vary. Possible answer: They are similar because they are both mothers and have daughters who play in the school orchestra. They are different because they have different views about age and weight. Mrs. Yang spends her days shopping and cooking, but Mrs. Hanson works in a hospital.

Page 48
1. C; 2. F; 3. A
4. Answers may vary. Possible answer: The narrator and Holly are both students in the school orchestra. They are different

because Holly is an only child with divorced parents, while the narrator lives with her parents, brothers, and sisters.
5. Answers may vary. Possible answer: They are similar because they both were immigrants from China who found it difficult to be an outsider in America.

Page 49
1. A; 2. H; 3. D
4. Students should conclude that the third sentence states the main idea. Explanations may vary slightly.

Page 50
1. C; 2. G; 3. B; 4. J
5. Answers may vary, but should recognize the main idea of this part of the story. Possible answer: Dusty is relaxed and confident because he is in the lead.

Page 51
1. C; 2. J; 3. C
4. Students should conclude that Dusty is making good time with the dogs. He is able to take a break to give the dogs a snack, and he can see that no one is behind him for at least five miles.
5. Answers may vary, but titles may include Dusty's name, as well as words like *Team* and *Obstacle*.

Page 52
1. B; 2. G; 3. C
4. Answers will vary, but should indicate an accurate evaluation of the information provided. Possible answer: They check the weather report first.

Page 53
1. B; 2. G; 3. A; 4. F
5. Answers may vary, but students will most likely conclude that he will be wiser for having learned that he should not be so reckless anymore.

Page 54
1. C; 2. G; 3. A
4. Students may mention feelings, such as fear and surprise, that Ohkwa'ri experienced, or they may relate events such as the encounter with the rattlesnake.
5. Answers will vary, but students should support their answers with evidence from both texts.

Page 55
1. B; 2. H; 3. A
4. Answers will vary, but they should mention the phrase "At the same time."

Page 56
1. C; 2. H; 3. A; 4. G
5. Answers may vary, but they should be related to the idea of a belief or tradition.

Page 57
1. C; 2. J; 3. B
4. Answers may vary, but they should acknowledge that the anchor runner is the team's last chance to make a final sprint and win. The anchor must be a strong, confident runner.
5. Answers will vary, but should demonstrate an ability to discern the meaning of an unknown word based on clues within the text.

Page 58
1. C; 2. J; 3. A
4. Students should conclude that the purpose was to inform someone about how to make spaghetti sauce.

Page 59
1. D; 2. F; 3. D; 4. G
5. Answers may vary, but students should generally conclude that the author is writing to inform people about Alzheimer's and to express the love between the family. This should be supported with examples.

Page 60
1. A; 2. J; 3. D
4. Answers may vary, but students will most likely say that the story made them sad because the author talks about the family sharing memories and spending time together.
5. Answers may vary, but they should include the definition of a memory box, as well as a clear and ordered set of persuasive points.

Page 61
1. A; 2. J; 3. B
4. Answers may vary, but they should indicate an understanding of story elements within the text.

Page 62
1. C; 2. J; 3. B; 4. G
5. Answers may vary. Possible answers: The illustrations show cars from the early 1900s. In addition, the clothes, streets, and buildings, as well as the inside of Lila's house, suggest the early 1900s in a large city.

Page 63
1. C; 2. G; 3. B
4. Answers may vary, but they should demonstrate a recognition and application of context clues. Most

students will conclude that it is New York City.
5. Answers may vary, but students should choose something that Lila would think worth fighting for, based on the information given about her personality.

Page 64
1. D; 2. F; 3. B
4. Answers may vary, but they should include major ideas from the article written in the students' own words.

Page 65
1. D; 2. J; 3. B; 4. G
5. Answers may vary, but they should include the main details from this section of the text, as well as an explanation of what happened.

Page 66
1. D; 2. G; 3. B
4. Answers may vary, but they should include main details. Possible answer: Mr. Garrett disguises Harriet in fancy clothes, gives her directions to Pennsylvania, and warns her to be careful.
5. Answers may vary, but they should indicate an understanding of paraphrasing.

Page 67
1. B; 2. J; 3. D
4. Answers will vary, but they should demonstrate an active, imaginative response to the literature, as well as identification of text clues to support description.

Page 68
1. B; 2. F; 3. C; 4. J
5. Answers may vary, but they should indicate a comprehension of visualization through the inclusion of vivid details and descriptive language from the text.

Page 69
1. A; 2. F; 3. D
4. Answers may vary, but they should include vivid details and vivid images from the text.
5. Answers may vary, but they should use descriptive language that provides enough detail for the reader to visualize the scene.

Page 70
1. A; 2. H; 3. D
4. Answers will vary, but they should use knowledge of word meanings and origins to determine the definition of the unknown word.

Page 71
1. D; 2. H; 3. B; 4. G
5. Answers may vary, but they should

© Scott Foresman 5

indicate an understanding of the word based on contextual clues given in the text.

Page 72
1. D; 2. H; 3. B
4. Answers may vary, but the student's selection should reflect comprehension of how to use context clues in order to discover the meaning of an unknown word.
5. Answers may vary, but they should indicate attention to and comprehension of contextual clues as well as clear examples from the story that sufficiently support the student's answer.

Page 73
1. B; 2. F; 3. D
4. Answers may vary, but students should be able to recognize main idea, recast the paragraph into their own words, and include the important points.

Page 74
1. C; 2. J; 3. A; 4. F
5. Answers may vary, but they should acknowledge that the farmers bravely pursued the British and caused them to flee.

Page 75
1. C; 2. F; 3. A
4. Answers will vary, but they might use imagination in recounting the historical facts and give the account a personal touch.
5. Answers will vary, but they should acknowledge the historical significance of Revere's ride.

Page 76
1. C; 2. G; 3. C
4. Students should conclude that there is no merit to being greedy. The explanation should effectively simplify the lesson.

Page 77
1. A; 2. J; 3. C; 4. J
5. Sentences should show that Manuel no longer values money above everything.

Page 78
1. D; 2. G; 3. A
4. Students should conclude that Manuel has learned that there are things more important than money.
5. Answers will vary, but they should be supported with concrete examples of what students consider the best things in life.

Page 79
1. A; 2. F; 3. C
4. Answers may vary, but they should mention an additional step, placed in the proper order.

Page 80
1. C; 2. H; 3. D; 4. J
5. Answers will vary, but most students will write about how Andy and his brownies would fit in perfectly at the Bug Bowl.

Page 81
1. D; 2. J; 3. A
4. Answers may vary slightly, but steps should be in sequential order based on information from the story.
5. Answers may vary, but they might include consulting a scientist familiar with bugs or reading articles such as "Bug-a-licious!"

Page 82
1. C; 2. J; 3. C
4. Answers may vary, but they should indicate an understanding that Hattie uses humor (sometimes a good way to resolve problems) in referring to the *other* turkey.

Page 83
1. D; 2. G; 3. A; 4. G
5. Answers may vary, but should indicate an understanding of the story's plot.

Page 84
1. D; 2. G; 3. A
4. Answers should acknowledge that the climax occurs when the young men discover that the old woman has tricked them.
5. Answers will vary. Fables such as "The Fox and the Crow" and stories such as "Stone Soup" involve trickery.

Page 85
1. A; 2. J; 3. A
4. Answers may vary, but Mei's mother has based her judgment on what has happened at Lili's house.

Page 86
1. B; 2. J; 3. D; 4. H
5. Answers may vary, but students may say that the author recognizes Felicia's good qualities yet still understand her flaws as an overly critical person.

Page 87
1. B; 2. J; 3. D
4. Answers may vary, but some students will say that Marilyn is overly concerned with how she looks.

5. Answers may vary. Some students may feel that someone as critical and outspoken as Felicia would not make a good friend. Others might think that she is loyal and willing to try to correct her flaws.

Page 88
1. D; 2. F; 3. B
4. Answers will vary, depending on students' preference for romantic garden scenes over other subject matter.

Page 89
1. B; 2. H; 3. D; 4. J
5. Answers will vary, but they should include information drawn from the scientific article, presented in sequential order.

Page 90
1. B; 2. J; 3. D
4. Answers may include words such as *crate, sad-faced,* and *sleepy.*
5. Answers should mention specific objects such as the paper airplane, feather, and notebook paper, and realistic details such as the ragged edge of the torn newspaper.

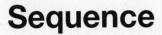

Reading Objective: Apply a variety of reading strategies.
Writing Objective: Begin to evaluate and revise writing to focus on purpose, organization, transition, and audience.

Name _____

Sequence

Sequence is the order in which things happen. Words such as *now, then, first, during, afterward,* **and** *while* **help you understand the sequence of events in a story.**

When Marta came home from soccer practice, she was really hungry. She decided to make her favorite snack, a peanut butter and raisin sandwich. First she put a slice of bread in the toaster. While the bread was toasting, she spilled a box of raisins all over the floor. While she was picking up the raisins, the toast burned. Then Marta put peanut butter on the burnt toast, but she dropped the whole thing, peanut butter-side down, on the floor. At last Marta finished cleaning the kitchen. By this time, she was too tired to eat and took a nap instead!

1 **What happens first in the story?**

A Marta puts peanut butter on the toast.

B Marta takes a nap.

C Marta puts a slice of bread in the toaster.

D Marta spills the raisins.

2 **Which event happens while the bread is in the toaster?**

F Marta spills the raisins.

G Marta drops the peanut butter sandwich.

H Marta cleans the kitchen.

J Marta takes a nap.

3 **Which answer best completes the empty box in the flow chart below?**

1. The bread goes in the toaster.	2. The toast burns.	3. ?	4. Marta drops the toast.

A Marta takes a nap.

B Marta decides to make a sandwich.

C Marta puts peanut butter on the toast.

D Marta opens the box of raisins.

4 **Write the steps you would take to make your favorite snack.**

_____

_____

_____

_____

_____

_____

_____

© Scott Foresman 5

Name _____

Sequence

Read "From the Diary of Leigh Botts" (pages 23–34). Then answer the questions below.

1 What event most likely happened to Leigh at school before the story begins?

A Other students made fun of his lunchbox.

B Someone took his diary.

C His teacher made him stay after school.

D Someone took part of his lunch.

2 What did Leigh do first to make his invention?

F He bought supplies.

G He installed the alarm in the lunchbox.

H He read books about batteries.

J He went to the hardware store.

3 On Saturday, March 3, which event happened last in the hardware store?

A Leigh learned that he needed a 6-volt battery.

B The man wished Leigh good luck.

C Leigh found a switch, battery, and doorbell.

D Leigh went to the hardware store.

4 Based on the steps that Leigh took to make his alarm, which word best describes his way of solving problems?

F lazy

G careful

H sloppy

J silly

5 Both Leigh and Alison DeSmyter, the inventor of the Rampanion (pages 37–39), solve problems by inventing things. What is the first step that a good problem–solver must take? Use Leigh and Alison as examples.

_____

_____

_____

_____

_____

_____

_____

_____

_____

Name _____

Sequence

Read "The Rampanion" (pages 37–39). Then answer the questions below.

1 How many ramp materials did Alison reject before she decided to use lightweight metal?

  A none

  B one

  C two

  D three

2 Read page 39. Before the Rampanion can be placed in the cloth carry bag,

  F it must be cleaned

  G it must be attached to the wheelchair

  H it must be used

  J it must be folded

3 Which of the following events did <u>not</u> happen after Alison won the fifth-grade grand prize?

  A She worked on the Handy Helper.

  B She visited the Kennedy Space Center.

  C She improved the Rampanion by putting sticky tape on the bottom.

  D She traveled to Florida.

4 Suppose you were in a wheelchair and needed to use the Rampanion to climb a curb. Based on what you know from the story, describe the steps you would take to use it.

_____

_____

_____

_____

5 Read "From The Diary of Leigh Botts" (pages 23–34). How are the themes of this selection and "The Rampanion" alike? Explain your answer.

_____

_____

_____

_____

© Scott Foresman 5

Tennessee

Name _____

Character

You can analyze a character in a story by understanding his or her thoughts, actions, words, and relationships with other characters. You may be asked on tests to describe or make judgments about that character.

> My dog Rufus makes such a scene in the morning. Even before I wake up, he is outside my room barking and scratching at the door. When I come out, he starts running around in circles and chasing his tail. Petting him makes him wag his stumpy tail. While I eat breakfast, he sits under my chair. As I leave the house to catch the bus for school, Rufus sits by the window and watches me go. When I return, he's right at the door waiting.

1 The word that best describes the dog Rufus is

A crazy

B loyal

C messy

D hungry

2 The most likely reason that Rufus chases his tail is because

F he is hungry

G he likes to play games

H he is confused

J he is happy to see his owner

3 Which answer best completes the empty box below?

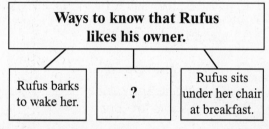

Ways to know that Rufus likes his owner.

| Rufus barks to wake her. | ? | Rufus sits under her chair at breakfast. |

A Rufus wags his tail.

B Rufus is a dog.

C Rufus likes to take walks.

D Rufus likes to eat her breakfast.

4 Write a paragraph from Rufus's point of view. Include the dog's thoughts, feelings, and actions as his owner gets ready for school.

_____

_____

_____

_____

_____

_____

Reading Objective: Develop skills in making inferences and recognizing unstated assumptions.
Writing Objective: Continue to respond actively and imaginatively to literature.

Tennessee

Name _____

Character

Read "Faith and Eddie" (pages 43–59). Then answer the questions below.

1 **When Faith returns home from school on pages 46–47, she feels**

A proud

B angry

C unhappy

D calm

2 **How does the reader know that Eddie is not like most dogs?**

F Eddie finds Faith when she is lost.

G Eddie learns to play the game "Fetch."

H Eddie learns to play Tug-of-War.

J Eddie gives Milagros a "beggar" face to get food.

3 **Eddie runs through the city without paying attention to the other dogs because**

A he is worried about finding Faith

B he does not like the other dogs

C he is angry that the other dogs will not speak to him

D he is afraid of the other dogs

4 **What is the main reason that Faith runs away?**

F She is looking for Eddie.

G She does not like the Spanish teacher, Coco.

H Her friends at school dare her to run away.

J She is lonely and sad living in her new home.

5 **What makes Eddie a good narrator for the story? Explain your answer.**

_____

_____

_____

_____

_____

_____

_____

_____

_____

Reading Objective: Develop skills in making inferences and recognizing unstated assumptions.
Writing Objective: Continue to respond actively and imaginatively to literature.

Tennessee

Name _____

Character

Read "Faith and Eddie" (pages 43–59). Then answer the questions below.

1 The word that best describes Coco's attitude towards Faith is

A bored

B patient

C strong

D angry

3 When he finds Faith, Eddie most likely feels

A relieved

B annoyed

C angry

D enraged

2 Which action shows that Faith is unhappy?

F She wears electric shoes.

G She dislikes Spanish lessons.

H She plays with Eddie after school.

J She comes home from school crying.

4 Choose one word to describe Faith's character. Then give three examples of Faith's thoughts, words, or actions to support your choice.

_____

_____

_____

_____

_____

5 Describe two ways that Eddie behaves like a dog and two ways that he behaves like a human.

_____

_____

_____

_____

_____

Tennessee

Reading Objective: Apply a variety of reading strategies.
Writing Objective: Use appropriate organizational strategies to develop writing.

Name _____

Generalizing

Generalizing is making a statement about what several people or things have in common. A generalization should be supported by facts and reason. Test questions asking for generalizations may include words such as *many, most, some* or *all*.

Some families are made up of parents and both adopted and birth children. The Sanders are one of those families. The parents, Tammy and Rob, did not think that Tammy could bear children. They spent many months preparing to adopt Bill, their oldest child. Two years later, Tammy gave birth to a child named Anna. Bill says that like most families, the Sanders share plenty of laughs and love.

1 **According to Bill, the characteristic that most families share is**

A adoption

B love

C children

D parents

2 **Which of the following generalizations is based on facts from the selection?**

F All families are made of parents and birth children.

G All adoptions take many months.

H Some families have both adopted and birth children.

J No families have both adopted and birth children.

3 **Which answer best completes the empty chart below?**

Children in the same family may have different birth parents.

Some children are adopted.	?

A Adopted and birth children may be raised in the same family.

B All children have parents.

C Friends are not biologically related.

D Some families have pets.

4 **Make a generalization about families. Support your idea with two facts.**

_____

_____

_____

_____

_____

_____

Reading Objective: Apply a variety of reading strategies.
Writing Objective: Use appropriate organizational strategies to develop writing.

Tennessee

Name _____

Generalizing

Read "Looking for a Home" (pages 65–76). Then answer the questions below.

1 On page 68, what generalization does the author make about what happened when the orphan train stopped?

   A Lee needed a haircut.

   B As usual, a crowd met the train and looked the children over.

   C A man and his wife adopted Gerald.

   D The children spent the night sleeping in a hotel.

2 Which statement from pages 74–75 best supports the generalization that Lee feels that adults are often upset with him?

   F "I had always felt like a bother to adults."

   G "I meant to run away that very night."

   H "I stole a glance at Ben."

   J "Then I started to listen to her."

3 The most important difference between Lee's experience with the Naillings and all other families is

   A he had a larger bedroom

   B there was more food to eat

   C he felt wanted by the family

   D he liked the house

4 According to this story, which of the following is a valid statement?

   F Older children were always chosen first.

   G Brothers and sisters usually ended up in the same family.

   H Life on the train was difficult for the children.

   J Children always fought with each other on the train.

5 Generalize about whether or not the Naillings will be good parents to Lee. Give examples from the story to support your argument.

_____

_____

_____

_____

_____

_____

_____

© Scott Foresman 5

Tennessee

Reading Objective: Apply a variety of reading strategies.
Writing Objective: Use appropriate organizational strategies to develop writing.

Name _____

Generalizing

Read "Looking for a Home" (pages 65–76). Then answer the questions below.

1 The word that best describes Lee's feelings toward his brothers is

A confused

B patient

C comfortable

D protective

2 Which statement from the story best supports the idea that Lee has bad feelings about the orphan train?

F "Lee and his brothers had been on the train more than a week. . . ."

G "Lee remembers a farmer . . . feeling his muscles."

H "I got back on the train that day with such a sense of dread. . . ."

J "No strangers were going to raise any of them."

3 Based on the breakfast scene described on pages 75–76, what can you say about the Naillings?

A They are wealthy.

B They care about Lee.

C They like Lee better than their own children.

D They are good eaters.

4 Describe how the children on the orphan train felt about their experience. Give at least three examples from the story to support your generalizations.

_____

_____

_____

_____

5 Do you like or dislike the Naillings? Explain.

_____

_____

_____

Tennessee

Reading Objective: Improve comprehension by interpreting, analyzing, synthesizing, and evaluating written text.

Writing Objective: Write frequently for a variety of purposes such as narration, description, and personal, creative expression.

Name _____

Cause and Effect

A cause is why something happens, and an effect is what happens. Test questions about cause and effect often include clue words such as *why, because,* or *since.*

The Bradford Bears had a good chance to score a run and win the game. The bases were loaded because the pitcher had walked the last batter, Bob. Karen, one of the fastest runners on the team, was on third base. José stood in the batter's box, waiting for the pitch. The pitcher threw a fastball right down the middle. José swung and hit the ball on the ground toward the shortstop. The shortstop had trouble getting a good grip on it. He finally threw the ball toward home plate as Karen raced to beat the throw. She slid into home. The catcher missed the tag. Karen scored. The Bears won the game!

1 **What causes the bases to be loaded?**

A The pitcher walks Bob.

B José hits a ground ball.

C Karen is a fast runner.

D Karen has to slide into home.

2 **The throw to home plate is late because**

F Karen runs fast and slides into home

G José hits a ground ball to the shortstop

H the bases are loaded

J the shortstop has trouble gripping the ball

3 **Which answer best completes the empty box below?**

Causes ⟶ Effect

| The shortstop has trouble fielding the ball. |
| Karen slides into home. | → | Karen scores a run. |
| ? |

A The pitcher throws a fastball.

B The pitcher walks Bob.

C The catcher misses the tag.

D The bases are loaded.

4 **Give at least three examples of causes that make it possible for the Bradford Bears to win the baseball game.**

_____

_____

_____

_____

Tennessee

Reading Objective: Improve comprehension by interpreting, analyzing, and evaluating written text.
Writing Objective: Write frequently for a variety of purposes such as narration, description, and personal, creative expression.

Name _____

Cause and Effect

Read "Meeting Mr. Henry" (pages 87–100). Then answer the questions below.

1 On pages 88–90, the main reason that Jason offers to take the bases down to the gym for Mr. Henry is to

A know if Mr. Henry thought he was out at first base

B avoid seeing the rest of the team

C to be helpful

D see Mr. Henry because he misses him

2 Jason makes an out rather than beat the throw to first base because

F he has a broken ankle

G he runs in the wrong direction

H he does not know that he is supposed to run

J he stays in the batter's box too long

3 According to Mr. Henry, which of the following statements is <u>not</u> a reason why Willie Mays was a great baseball player?

A He could run very fast.

B He was sixteen when he played for the Birmingham Black Barons.

C He could throw runners out from deep center field.

D He was a strong hitter.

4 What statement best describes the effect that Mr. Henry will have on Jason when he plays for his new team?

F Jason will always collect the bases after a game.

G Jason will become a pitcher on the team.

H Jason will be a more confident player.

J Jason will run faster.

5 Mr. Henry tells Jason many stories about the history of baseball, especially about African-American players and the Negro League. What effect is he trying to have on Jason?

_____

_____

_____

_____

_____

_____

_____

Reading Objective: Improve comprehension by interpreting, analyzing, and evaluating written text.
Writing Objective: Write frequently for a variety of purposes such as narration, description, and personal, creative expression.

Tennessee

Name _____

Cause and Effect

Read "Meeting Mr. Henry" (pages 87–100). Then answer the questions below.

1 Jason stays in the batter's box for so long because

  A he is angry with his team and decides not to run

  B he watches the ball before running to first base

  C he does not know the rules of baseball

  D he is unable to run faster

2 Which of the following events does <u>not</u> cause Jason to feel more excited about baseball at the end of the story?

  F He will be on a new team.

  G He hears stories about great players of the past.

  H He practices with Mr. Henry.

  J He learns how to see without looking.

3 What main effect does Mr. Henry have by comparing Jason to Willie Mays and Roy Campanella?

  A Jason runs faster.

  B Jason wants to work with Mr. Henry.

  C Jason feels more confident.

  D Jason decides to become a professional baseball player.

4 When Jason and Mr. Henry play imaginary baseball on pages 97–98, Mr. Henry seems to become younger to Jason. What causes this to happen?

_____

_____

_____

_____

5 Choose one character. How is this character important to the story?

_____

_____

_____

_____

Reading Objective: Read independently for a variety of purposes.
Writing Objective: Begin to evaluate and revise writing to focus on purpose, organization, transition, and audience.

Name _____

Author's Purpose

An author's purpose is the reason the author wrote the story. The author's purpose may be to inform, persuade, express feelings or beliefs, or entertain the reader. Test questions that ask about why or how a story is written may be asking for author's purpose.

Landfills are giant holes in the ground where trash is buried. Nearly one-third of the trash in landfills is paper that has been thrown away rather than recycled. There are many things that people can do to help prevent paper waste. First, people can buy products that have less packaging. Paper, especially office paper, can be reused and then recycled. Finally, consumers can buy products that are made from recycled paper. All of these steps will help reduce the amount of trash that goes into landfills.

1 The main reason that the author wrote this paragraph is to

A teach people about where trash goes

B sell recycled paper products

C help people save money

D show how to reduce the amount of trash

2 The sentence in the paragraph that best states what the author is trying to say is

F the first sentence

G the third sentence

H the fifth sentence

J the last sentence

3 Which answer best completes the chart below?

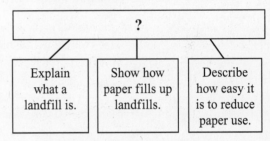

A Argue for more landfills.

B Tell people how to make less paper waste.

C Help people save money.

D Influence the town council.

4 Brainstorm three ways you can cut down on paper waste in your own life.

_____

_____

_____

_____

_____

_____

Tennessee

Name _____

Author's Purpose

Read "Eloise Greenfield" (pages 105–116). Then answer the questions below.

1 **Which word best describes the author's memories of her childhood?**

A confused

B fond

C angry

D sad

2 **The author wrote this passage because**

F she wants the readers to know her background

G she is selfish

H she is trying to remember the name of her home

J her parents made her write about them

3 **Why does the author talk about her family's visits to Langston Terrace before they moved in?**

A to inform the reader about how a building is constructed

B to show how excited her family was to have a new home

C to tell about her earliest memories

D to help the reader visualize what her family looked like

4 **The author most likely wrote the story as an autobiography because**

F she does not know how to write fiction stories

G she wants to share her own experiences with others

H she wants to express her sadness about her life

J she wants people to know how to buy a home

5 **Why do you think the author included pictures in her autobiography?**

_____

_____

_____

_____

_____

_____

_____

_____

© Scott Foresman 5

Reading Objective: Read independently for a variety of purposes.
Writing Objective: Begin to evaluate and revise writing to focus on purpose, organization, transition, and audience.

Name _____

Author's Purpose

Read "Eloise Greenfield" (pages 105–116). Then answer the questions below.

1 The author's purpose is to

  A make the reader laugh

  B convince people to live at Langston Terrace

  C impress the readers with her extraordinary life

  D share her experiences growing up with others

2 Read page 112. What did the author mean when she described Langston Terrace as an "in-between" place?

  F It was a good place to live until people could buy their own homes.

  G It was located between her old apartment and where she went to school.

  H It was between the library and the new playground.

  J It was built between the play and the author's birthday.

3 Langston Terrace was a good "growing-up place" for the author because

  A life was perfect there

  B rents were cheap

  C there was a resident council

  D there were good neighbors, families, and many fun things to do

4 On page 110, why does the author describe her mother's visits to Langston Terrace construction site?

_____

_____

_____

5 What special words did the author use to help you see, hear, and feel things in this story?

_____

_____

_____

_____

© Scott Foresman 5

Tennessee

Reading Objective: Apply a variety of reading strategies.
Writing Objective: Use elements of the writing process as appropriate to the writing task.

Name _____

Steps in a Process

Test questions that ask you to explain how to perform an action may be asking for the steps in a process. Look for words such as *first* and *next* and try to picture the steps or the results to help you understand a process.

According to the National Safety Council, drowning kills about 4,800 Americans each year. You don't have to be a lifeguard to help reduce that number. The first thing you should always do if a person appears to be drowning is to have someone call 911 and alert any lifeguards and adults. Then, there are four basic steps you can take to help: reach, throw, row, and go. Reach: First, use a lightweight pole, long stick, or ladder—anything that can extend your reach. Throw: If you cannot reach the person, find something that floats to throw out. If rope is available, tie it to an object before you throw it so you can get it back. Row: Then, if the victim is still out of reach and a boat, boogie board, or some such thing is available, you might try to "row" to him or her. When you do get to the victim, don't try to pull him or her in over the side of the boat. This could cause it to capsize. Pull the person in at the stern, or rear end. Go: Finally, if nothing else works, you must determine whether you are a strong enough swimmer to enter the water and go to the drowning person. You should attempt to go to the person only if you have been trained in lifesaving techniques.

1 **What is the first thing you should do if you see someone drowning?**

A Swim out to save the person.

B Tie a rope around a floating object.

C Reach out to the victim with a long object.

D Have someone call for help.

2 **Right after you row out to a drowning victim, you should**

F pull him or her in over the side

G tie a rope to a floating object

H pull him or her in at the stern

J jump out of the boat and swim

3 **Which answer best completes the list of events shown below?**

How to Help a Drowning Victim
1. Reach out to the victim.
2. ?
3. Row to the victim in a boat.

A Learn lifesaving techniques.

B Find some rope.

C Throw something that floats.

D Swim out to the victim.

4 Imagine you saw someone having trouble swimming in a pond. Tell what steps you would take to help him or her get safely back to land.

_____

_____

_____

Name _____

Steps in a Process

Read "The Diver and the Dolphins" (pages 127–140). Then answer the questions below.

1 In this story, what process is being described?

A Wayne Grover's attempt to find a new home for a family of dolphins

B Wayne Grover's attempt to find an orphaned dolphin's parents

C Wayne Grover's attempt to save a baby dolphin that has been hurt

D Wayne Grover's attempt to fight off sharks

2 What does Wayne Grover do first in attempting to help the baby dolphin?

F He makes his own clicking noises.

G He strokes it.

H He starts pulling the embedded line.

J He removes the hook.

3 What is the last step Wayne Grover takes before he lets the dolphin go?

A He wraps the wound in a bandage.

B He holds the dolphin down with his leg.

C He removes the hook from the wound.

D He presses on the wound to stop the bleeding.

4 The father dolphin does all of the following things to help the baby dolphin except

F hit the bigger shark

G push the diver's arm with his nose

H carry the baby dolphin on his back

J make clicking noises to attract the diver

5 Read "Dolphin Behavior" (pages 143–145). How did the dolphins in "The Diver and the Dolphins" behave similarly to the typical dolphin behavior you learned about?

_____

_____

_____

_____

_____

_____

_____

_____

_____

_____

Reading Objective: Apply a variety of reading strategies.
Writing Objective: Use elements of the writing process as appropriate to the writing task.

Tennessee

Name _____

Steps in a Process

Read "Dolphin Behavior" (pages 143–145). Then answer the questions below.

1 What must researchers do first when they study dolphin behavior?

A feed them

B approach them

C identify individual dolphins

D report on how they live

2 What happens after researchers identify the dolphins?

F They make sound recordings.

G They name them.

H They take photos.

J They write descriptions.

3 How long do dolphins spend in a nursery group?

A six months

B one year

C three years

D their whole lives

4 Write the steps you would take to study a group of dolphins.

_____

_____

_____

_____

_____

5 Summarize the steps a dolphin takes as it is growing up in a dolphin society.

_____

_____

_____

_____

_____

Reading Objective: Improve comprehension by interpreting and evaluating written text.
Writing Objective: Write to acquire knowledge, clarify thinking, and improve study skills.

Tennessee

Name _____

Graphic Sources

Sometimes important information in a story is given in the form of graphics such as diagrams, graphs, and pictures. Look at these graphic sources in order to interpret information quickly.

The U.S. Weather Service uses something called the Beaufort Scale to measure wind speeds. Use this chart to answer the questions.

Scale Number	Wind Condition	Wind Speed in Miles Per Hour
1	Calm	under 1 mph
2	Light Air	1–3 mph
3	Light Breeze	4–7 mph
4	Gentle Breeze	8–12 mph
5	Moderate Breeze	13–18 mph
6	Fresh Breeze	19–24 mph
7	Strong Breeze	25–31 mph
8	Near Gale	32–38 mph
9	Gale	39–46 mph
10	Strong Gale	47–54 mph
11	Storm	55–63 mph
12	Violent Storm	64–72 mph
13	Hurricane	over 72 mph

1 The U.S. Weather Service call winds with a speed of 27 mph

A a hurricane

B a strong breeze

C a near gale

D a storm

2 What are the wind conditions when the scale number is 2?

F a light air

G a gale

H a storm

J a hurricane

3 According to the chart, what is the lowest wind speed that is considered a hurricane?

A 71

B 72

C 73

D 74

4 Describe something you could do outside on a day that measured 4 on the Beaufort Scale.

_____

_____

_____

Tennessee

Reading Objective: Improve comprehension by interpreting and evaluating written text.
Writing Objective: Write to acquire knowledge, clarify thinking, and improve study skills.

Name _____

Graphic Sources

Read "The Fury of a Hurricane" (pages 149–162). Then answer the questions below.

1 According to the diagram on page 151, what weather element rises to begin forming a hurricane?

A cold rain

B tall clouds

C warm air

D thunderstorms

2 Look at the diagram on page 152. Suppose a hurricane first has winds blowing from east to west. After the eye passes, the winds will blow

F east to west

G west to east

H north to south

J south to north

3 Which statement best describes the purpose of the photographs on pages 156, 157, and 159?

A They show how hurricanes are formed.

B They show how people should behave during a hurricane.

C They show the environment of the Everglades.

D They show the possible effects of a hurricane.

4 According to the diagrams on page 161, which type of environment shows the most growth in South Florida from around 1871 to today?

F cypress swamplands

G Everglades

H urban areas

J agricultural lands

5 Read "Flying into a Hurricane" (pages 165–167) and study the illustrations and caption. Then explain in your own words why hurricanes today are less deadly than earlier ones.

_____

_____

_____

_____

_____

_____

_____

_____

Tennessee

Reading Objective: Improve comprehension by interpreting, and evaluating written text.
Writing Objective: Write to acquire knowledge, clarify thinking, and improve study skills.

Name _____

Graphic Sources

Read "The Fury of a Hurricane" (pages 149–162). Then answer the questions below.

1 According to the maps on page 161, all of the areas existed in South Florida around 1871 except

  A the water conservation area

  B the Everglades

  C the coastal marshes and mangrove swamps

  D the prairie grasslands

2 According to the diagram on page 153, which of the following is <u>not</u> inside a hurricane?

  F tail winds

  G warm air

  H low pressure area

  J ocean surface

3 Look at the diagram on page 153. What do you call the center part of a hurricane where the air is calm?

  A dome

  B tail

  C eye

  D eye wall

4 Study the diagram and caption on page 151 that tell how a hurricane is born. Describe this process in your own words.

_____

_____

_____

_____

5 Read "Flying into a Hurricane" (pages 165–167). Compare the graphics to those in "The Fury of a Hurricane." Which do you find more useful or more interesting? Explain.

_____

_____

_____

_____

Tennessee

Reading Objective: Develop skills in making inferences and recognizing unstated assumptions.
Reading Objective: Improve comprehension by analyzing and evaluating written text.

Name _____

Fact and Opinion

Remember that a fact can be proven true or false, but an opinion cannot. Look for words such as *wonderful, best, worst, should,* and *everyone* that may signal opinions in test questions. Keep in mind that if someone could reasonably disagree with a statement, it is not a fact.

  Charlie prepared sandwiches for the homeless shelter in his town. He thought that he could help less fortunate people by providing them with tasty food. During the weekend, he would make 50 ham, 40 tuna, and 30 turkey sandwiches. He made more ham sandwiches because ham cost less, but tuna tasted best. Each week when he delivered the sandwiches, he received many thanks from the people at the shelter. Charlie says that being hungry is the worst feeling in the world. All the people at the shelter think Charlie is the nicest kid they know.

1   **Which choice best describes the fourth sentence of this paragraph?**

 A   fact

 B   opinion

 C   fact and opinion

 D   neither fact nor opinion

2   **How could you check if the statement that Charlie makes 50 ham, 40 tuna, and 30 turkey sandwiches is true?**

 F   Ask the people at the shelter if they liked the sandwiches.

 G   Make the sandwiches yourself and count them.

 H   Reread the first sentence.

 J   Visit Charlie and count the sandwiches.

3   **Which word best completes the empty box in the chart below?**

Words That Indicate Opinions		
nicest	best	?

 A   sandwiches

 B   cost

 C   many

 D   worst

4   **Select and write one fact and one opinion from the paragraph. Explain how you know which is a fact and which is an opinion.**

_____

_____

_____

_____

_____

_____

Reading Objective: Develop skills in making inferences and recognizing unstated assumptions.
Reading Objective: Improve comprehension by analyzing and evaluating written text.

Tennessee

Name _____

Fact and Opinion

Read "Dwaina Brooks" (pages 171–181). Then answer the questions below.

1 Which choice best describes the statement that 23 classmates helped Dwaina make meals for the homeless?

A fact

B opinion

C fact and opinion

D neither fact nor opinion

2 Which sentence states a fact?

F People should help each other.

G Dwaina is a good person.

H Dwaina will be the best doctor in Dallas when she grows up.

J There are hundreds of homeless people in Dallas.

3 Which of the following statements is an opinion?

A Kids should help the homeless.

B Dwaina and her classmates made over 300 meals in one night.

C Dwaina's mother and sisters helped her make sandwiches.

D The sandwiches and meals helped feed the homeless.

4 Which statement is a valid statement based on the facts in the story?

F Most people who help the homeless were once homeless themselves.

G Many homeless people once had homes and jobs.

H Most homeless people like sandwiches best.

J All children help the homeless.

5 Explain which of the following sentences is a fact and which are opinions. Give reasons for your explanations.

(1) The greatest thing kids can do is to help people. (2) In my opinion, all kids will be better adults if they care about others. (3) Today, there are over 300 organizations in the United States that kids can join to help others.

_____

_____

_____

_____

_____

_____

_____

Reading Objective: Develop skills in making inferences and recognizing unstated assumptions.
Reading Objective: Improve comprehension by analyzing and evaluating written text.

Tennessee

Name _____

Fact and Opinion

Read "Dwaina Brooks" (pages 171–181). Then answer the questions below.

1 Which sentence states a fact?

A More homeless people should have jobs.

B Everyone loves Dwaina.

C Dwaina will be the best doctor in Dallas when she grows up.

D There are thirty homeless shelters in Dallas.

2 All of the following are facts except

F that kids should help the homeless

G that Dwaina and her classmates made over 300 meals in one night

H that Dwaina's mother and sisters helped her make sandwiches

J that the sandwiches and meals helped feed the homeless

3 Choose the word that signals an opinion in this sentence: "Dwaina hopes to become a doctor someday, but she thinks it's crazy to wait till then to start caring for others."

A caring

B thinks

C someday

D wait

4 Find one fact and one opinion on pages 180–181. Explain how you can tell which is a fact and which is an opinion.

_____

_____

_____

_____

5 On page 179, Dwaina states that homelessness is getting worse. Is this statement a fact or an opinion? Explain how you can defend your answer.

_____

_____

_____

_____

© Scott Foresman 5

Reading Objective: Use comprehension strategies to enhance understanding and to respond to literature.

Tennessee

Name _____

Author's Viewpoint

Some passages in tests will contain opinions and words that indicate the author's point of view. Sometimes authors indicate their viewpoint with words or phrases such as *must* and *I think*. At other times, you will have to read closely to find out if the author is expressing personal feelings.

People must do more than talk about the problems with the environment. I believe we must do something to guard our environment. Everyone can make less trash by recycling paper and buying recycled paper and plastic products. We can also save water by taking shorter showers and turning off the water when we brush our teeth. If we all make just a few small changes in our lifestyle, the effect on the environment could be enormous. Start today!

1 **Which sentence in the paragraph best describes the author's viewpoint?**

A second

B third

C fourth

D last

2 **What is the author mostly trying to say?**

F The environment has many problems that should be discussed.

G Helping the environment requires major changes in everyone's life.

H If we all make small changes in our lives, we can have a great effect on the environment.

J There is very little that people can do to help the environment.

3 **Which answer best completes the chart below?**

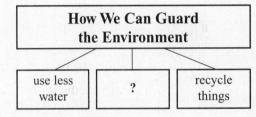

A drive carefully

B eat more fruit

C attend school regularly

D waste less paper

4 **Choose two words, phrases, or sentences in the paragraph that help explain the author's viewpoint. Explain how they show you what the author is trying to say.**

_____

_____

_____

_____

_____

Name _____

Author's Viewpoint

Read *Everglades* (pages 187–198). Then answer the questions below.

1 Which word best describes how the author feels about what has happened to the Everglades?

A calm

B confused

C sad

D joyful

2 The main reason that the author wrote this story is to

F show people how to go boating in the Everglades

G give a list of the plants and animals that live in the Everglades

H promote tourism in the Everglades

J show people what has happened today to the Everglades

3 Why does the author tell the "happy" story after the sad story?

A to show that there is hope for the Everglades if people care

B to make people happy and sell more books

C to continue the story about the Everglades

D because the boat ride is not over yet

4 What can you tell about the author of this story?

F She believes that there is no hope for the Everglades.

G She loves the natural world and is concerned about its survival.

H She wants to live in the Everglades.

J She prefers to tell happy stories.

5 The "new story" on page 198 clearly shows the author's viewpoint without using words like *should*. How does the author present her viewpoint through the children who are eager to grow up?

_____

_____

_____

_____

_____

_____

_____

_____

© Scott Foresman 5

Reading Objective: Use comprehension strategies to enhance understanding and to respond to literature.
Writing Objective: Use appropriate organizational strategies to develop writing.

Tennessee

Name _____

Author's Viewpoint

Read *Everglades* (pages 187–198). Then answer the questions below.

1 The author probably wants readers to feel all of the following except

A concern

B wonder

C boredom

D sadness

2 Which of the following is <u>not</u> part of the author's purpose in writing this article?

F to present hope for the future of the Everglades

G to portray the former beauty of the Everglades

H to show people what has happened to the Everglades

J to promote tourism in the Everglades

3 Which of the following is closest to the author's viewpoint?

A Conquistadors ruined the Everglades.

B Nobody should visit the Everglades.

C More people should live in the Everglades.

D The plants and animals of the Everglades can return only if people change their ways.

4 In the author's view, the Everglades was one of the most beautiful areas in the United States. Find three descriptions you like that show this beauty and tell why you like them.

_____

_____

_____

_____

5 Read "Florida Everglades" (pages 202–203), which is a nonfiction account. *Everglades* is a fictional account. Compare their messages about saving the Everglades. Explain your answer.

_____

_____

_____

_____

Reading Objective: Develop skills in making inferences and recognizing unstated assumptions.
Reading Objective: Use comprehension strategies to enhance understanding, to make predictions, and to respond to literature.

Tennessee

Name _____

Drawing Conclusions

Sometimes you will be asked to draw a conclusion. This means you will make a decision about something that is not actually stated in the text. You may have to go back to look for clues in a story to help you draw a conclusion.

The small package was wrapped in bright paper with a giant bow around it. There was a big card attached to it with my name on it. I lifted it up to see how it felt. It weighed about a pound, or as much as a big paperback book. I shook the box. Inside I could hear many smaller pieces rattling around. They shook together to make a clinking noise. It sounded like many pieces of smooth glass rubbing together. My mother said, "Be careful or you will break it." I looked at her and smiled from ear to ear. As soon as my friends and family finished singing, I opened that box first!

1 The narrator probably smiled "from ear to ear" because

A he or she thinks the gift is broken

B he or she likes surprises

C he or she thinks the gift is a paperback book

D he or she knows what is in the box

2 Which object is the best guess of what is inside the box?

F a basketball

G a puppy

H a set of marbles

J a new book

3 Which answer best completes the diagram shown below?

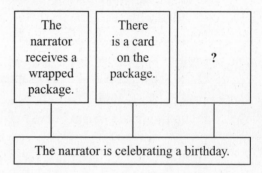

A The package weighs about one pound.

B The box has smaller pieces in it.

C The mother worries that the package will break.

D Friends and family sing before the present is opened.

4 Explain how you came to the conclusion that helped you answer Question 2.

_____

_____

_____

_____

_____

_____

© Scott Foresman 5

Tennessee

Reading Objective: Develop skills in making inferences and recognizing unstated assumptions.
Reading Objective: Use comprehension strategies to enhance understanding, to make predictions, and to respond to literature.

Name _____

Drawing Conclusions

Read "Missing Links" (pages 207–218). Then answer the questions below.

1 The stolen jewelry was most likely hidden

A in the sprinkler room

B in the baker's hat

C in the loaf of bread

D in Sherlock's éclair

2 Which fact helps the reader conclude that the baker is **not** very smart?

F He sells Amanda two loaves of bread.

G He wears the sapphire ring.

H He makes very heavy loaves of bread.

J He lets the bread get wet when the sprinklers are turned on.

3 Which of the following clues does **not** help Amanda and Sherlock solve the mystery?

A the rust-colored spot on the jewelry man's tie

B the fact that the sprinkler room is near the bakery

C the 15 pound loaf of bread

D the beauty of the sapphire ring

4 Which fact best supports the conclusion that Sherlock will make a good detective?

F He carries a magnifying glass.

G He notices small clues that help solve mysteries.

H He has the same first name as Sherlock Holmes, the great detective.

J He gets plenty of help from Amanda.

5 What conclusions can you draw about Amanda's and Sherlock's characters based on the events of this story? Give specific examples to support your conclusions.

_____

_____

_____

_____

_____

_____

_____

_____

© Scott Foresman 5

Tennessee

Reading Objective: Develop skills in making inferences and recognizing unstated assumptions.
Reading Objective: Use comprehension strategies to enhance understanding, to make predictions, and to respond to literature.

Name _____

Drawing Conclusions

Read "Missing Links" (pages 207–218). Then answer the questions below.

1 The picture on page 215 shows that the loaf of bread weighs 15 pounds. What conclusion do Amanda and Sherlock reach from this fact?

  A The baker makes very good bread.

  B They do not have enough money to buy the bread.

  C Something may be hidden in the bread.

  D They need to buy only one loaf.

2 Which of the following clues does <u>not</u> help Amanda and Sherlock solve the mystery?

  F the smudge on the salesman's chin

  G the fact that the jewelry salesman looks at his watch

  H the baker's refusal to sell Amanda the loaf of bread

  J the smell of the bakery

3 After reading the story, you could conclude that Sherlock

  A will get in a fight with his sister

  B will make a good detective

  C could never solve a mystery on his own

  D doesn't like bread

4 Imagine that Amanda and Sherlock go back to the department store the next day to buy the tie. Draw some conclusions about what they notice that is different from the day before.

_____

_____

_____

5 If your bike or something else valuable had been stolen, would you want Sherlock to investigate? Draw some conclusions about his character to explain why or why not.

_____

_____

_____

Name _____

Character

Test questions about character may ask you to describe or make judgments about a person in the story. You can find clues about characters by understanding their thoughts, actions, words, and relationships with other characters.

"...28, 29, 30." Monday, Luz shot 30 free throws after basketball practice. She decided to work on that shot because it was giving her trouble in the last game. Afterwards she played a game at the playground with her older sister and her friends. They were good players, and Luz had to work hard to keep up with them. Tuesday after practice she watched a game on TV to see how the pros play in a game situation. "Basketball can be hard work, but it will be worth it if I make the team," she thought excitedly.

1 All of the following describe Luz's feelings about basketball except

A devoted

B eager

C excited

D bored

2 Based on the way Luz practices basketball, which sentence best describes her character?

F She cares mostly about friends and family.

G She is a nervous person.

H She works hard to reach a goal.

J She wants to be a professional basketball player.

3 Which answer best completes the empty box shown below?

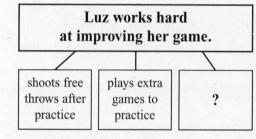

A talks about basketball a lot

B wears a nice looking uniform

C watches professional players

D does not complain about basketball practice

4 Describe Luz. Which clues in the story help you understand her character?

_____

_____

_____

_____

_____

_____

Reading Objective: Improve comprehension by interpreting, analyzing, and synthesizing written text.
Writing Objective: Write frequently for a variety of purposes such as description.

Tennessee

Name _____

Character

Read *Going with the Flow* (pages 229–240). Then answer the questions below.

1 Which word best describes how Mark feels about going to a new school?

A scared

B excited

C happy

D certain

2 On page 231, what does Mark's conversation with Mrs. LaVoie tell about how he feels?

F He does not like Mrs. LaVoie and wants a new translator.

G He is a bad student and will go only to gym.

H He resents moving to a new home and going to a new school.

J He is glad his dad found a new job.

3 How does Mark show Keith that he is not a wimp?

A He trips Keith.

B He speaks loudly.

C He plays basketball and runs very fast.

D He refuses to go with the flow.

4 Keith wants Mark to try out for the basketball team because

F he feels sorry for Mark

G he wants to learn sign language

H he promised Mark's mother he would be nice to him

J he thinks Mark is a good player

5 Explain how learning to go with the flow changes Mark.

_____

_____

_____

_____

_____

_____

_____

_____

_____

_____

Name _____

Character

Read *Going with the Flow* **(pages 229–240). Then answer the questions below.**

1 **Read page 230. How does Mark most likely feel?**

A excited

B embarrassed

C encouraged

D tired

2 **What does Mark's father ask him to do?**

F Stay a week to give the school a chance.

G Forget Jamie and make new friends.

H Join the basketball team.

J Teach the other students sign language.

3 **Keith does all of the following to show he is Mark's friend except**

A take notes for Mark

B invite him to play basketball

C lend him some lunch money

D tell him to go with the flow

4 **Explain how Mark's experience with Keith and the basketball team changes how he feels about the new school.**

_____

_____

_____

_____

5 **Explain what Mark discovers about Keith during the story. Which events in the story reveal Keith's character?**

_____

_____

_____

_____

Tennessee

Reading Objective: Improve comprehension by interpreting, analyzing, and synthesizing written text.
Writing Objective: Use elements of the writing process as appropriate to the writing task.

Name _____

Graphic Sources

Sometimes test questions will ask about information that is given in the form of graphic sources such as diagrams, graphs, or pictures. Study these graphics, along with captions or headings, in order to interpret information quickly.

Train companies organize and publish train schedules. These schedules make it possible to know when a train leaves one city and arrives at another. The schedule below shows the train stops between Astor and Elmond.

City	Train Arrives	Train Leaves
Astor	—	2:25 P.M.
Barnaby	2:42 P.M.	2:47 P.M.
Chisholm	3:10 P.M.	3:20 P.M.
Dooley	3:55 P.M.	4:18 P.M.
Elmond	4:36 P.M.	—

1 **What time does the train leave from Astor?**

A 2:25 P.M.

B 2:42 P.M.

C 2:47 P.M.

D The train does not leave from Astor.

2 **What time does the train arrive at Dooley?**

F 3:20 P.M.

G 3:55 P.M.

H 4:18 P.M.

J 4:36 P.M.

3 **How long does the train wait at the station in Barnaby?**

A 2 minutes

B 3 minutes

C 5 minutes

D The train does not stop in Barnaby.

4 **Suppose you wanted to take the 2:47 P.M. train from Barnaby to Dooley. If there were no delays, could you be in Dooley by 4:00 P.M.? Explain.**

_____

_____

_____

_____

© Scott Foresman 5

Reading Objective: Improve comprehension by interpreting, analyzing, and synthesizing written text.
Writing Objective: Use elements of the writing process as appropriate to the writing task.

Tennessee

Name _____

Graphic Sources

Read *Kate Shelley: Bound for Legend* (pages 245–260). Then answer the questions below.

1 Which river separates the Shelley home from the train station?

A Honey Creek

B Des Moines River

C Mill Creek

D Moingona

2 A train from Des Moines River Bridge to the Honey Creek Bridge travels

F north

G south

H east

J west

3 Imagine you are going from Boone to the Moingona station. How many bridges would you cross, according to the map on page 246?

A two

B three

C four

D five

4 How does the picture on page 254 help explain the action in the story?

F It shows how a tree fell onto the train tracks.

G It shows how rain makes lightning.

H It shows how dangerous it is to travel on trains in the rain.

J It shows how dangerous it was for Kate to cross the bridge.

5 Use the map on page 246. Describe what a train traveler on the Chicago & North Western Railroad would see from a passenger window. Start at the far east side of the map and travel west past the Mill Creek Bridge.

_____

_____

_____

_____

_____

_____

_____

_____

Reading Objective: Improve comprehension by interpreting, analyzing, and synthesizing, written text.
Writing Objective: Use elements of the writing process as appropriate to the writing task.

Tennessee

Name _____

Graphic Sources

Read *Kate Shelley: Bound for Legend* (pages 245–260). Then answer the questions below.

1 If a train were to travel east from Moingona, what would be the next town?

A Ogden

B Des Moines

C Boone

D Honey Creek

2 How many bridges are between the Shelley house and Moingona station?

F four

G three

H two

J one

3 According to the map on page 246, a train traveling from Moingona station to Ogden is moving

A northeast

B southeast

C southwest

D northwest

4 Name a type of graphic used in "The Last Western Frontier" (pages 263–265). Explain how this graphic helps you understand the events in the story.

_____

_____

_____

_____

_____

5 Compare the graphics from *Kate Shelley: Bound for Legend* with the graphics from "The Last Western Frontier." Which story do you think has more informative or interesting graphic sources? Explain.

_____

_____

_____

_____

_____

Reading Objective: Read independently for a variety of purposes.
Writing Objective: Write frequently for a variety of purposes such as narration, description, and personal creative expression.

Tennessee

Name _____

Plot

Test questions may ask about a story's plot, or important events. Look for the conflict, or main problem, at the beginning of a story and think about how it is resolved.

Jimmy's sister, Roshanda, wanted to ride a two-wheeled bike—without training wheels. But every time she tried, she just wobbled and fell. One day, Jimmy took her and her bike to the high school parking lot. They left the training wheels at home. "The main trick is to balance yourself," he told her. They practiced for hours. At first he held the bike and ran beside Roshanda as she rode. Then she kept her balance and he let go. Suddenly, she was riding! She rode around the parking lot six times without falling. Jimmy jogged beside her as she rode home without wobbling or falling down—and without training wheels.

1 **What is Roshanda's main problem in the story?**

A She has injuries from a fall from her bike.

B She is afraid of starting high school.

C Her brother is mean to her.

D She cannot ride a two-wheeled bike.

2 **Jimmy does all of the following to help solve Roshanda's problem except**

F leave her training wheels at home

G buy her candy

H practice with her for hours

J run beside her holding the bike

3 **What is the outcome of the story?**

A Roshanda has trouble riding her bike.

B Roshanda practices in the parking lot.

C Roshanda was able to ride home on her own.

D Jimmy and Roshanda go to the high school.

4 **Write about a time when you solved a problem. Describe the conflict and how it was solved.**

_____

_____

_____

_____

_____

_____

Tennessee

Reading Objective: Read independently for a variety of purposes.
Writing Objective: Write frequently for a variety of purposes such as narration, description, and personal creative expression.

Name _____

Plot

Read "The Marble Champ" (pages 269–280). Then answer the questions below.

1 What problem is Lupe trying to solve in this story?

A She is a poor student.

B She is a poor athlete.

C She does not have any trophies.

D Her brother does everything better than she does.

2 Which of the following events does not help Lupe solve her problem?

F She exercises her thumb by squeezing an eraser.

G She practices playing marbles.

H She buys a new set of marbles.

J She learns from her brother.

3 Which choice best describes the climax, or high point, of this story?

A Lupe practices a lot and shows that she is a determined person.

B Lupe tries her best in the championship and acts like a good sport.

C Lupe eats pizza and gets a good night's sleep after the tournament.

D Lupe wins the girl's division and defeats the winner of the boy's division.

4 What is the outcome that follows the climax?

F Lupe celebrates her success with her family.

G Lupe wins many more championships.

H Lupe goes home to practice more.

J Lupe becomes a friend to the girl in the baseball cap.

5 Describe a possible outcome of this story if Lupe had not won the championship.

_____

_____

_____

_____

_____

_____

_____

_____

© Scott Foresman 5

Tennessee

Reading Objective: Read independently for a variety of purposes.
Writing Objective: Write frequently for a variety of purposes such as narration, description, and personal creative expression.

Name _____

Plot

Read "The Marble Champ" (pages 269–280). Then answer the questions below.

1 **What is the best statement of the conflict at the beginning of the story?**

A Lupe never succeeds at anything she tries.

B Lupe does not do well in school.

C Lupe wants to win a sports contest.

D Lupe's brother does everything better than she does.

2 **Which of the following is not part of the rising action of the story?**

F Lupe does thumb exercises with an eraser and fingertip push-ups.

G Lupe practices with her brother.

H Lupe beats Alfonso the neighborhood champ.

J Lupe soaks her thumb in water and is thankful for winning.

3 **The climax of this story is when**

A Lupe makes it to the championship and wins

B Lupe practices constantly for two weeks

C Lupe celebrates her success with her family

D Lupe beats both her brother and Alfonso

4 **Summarize the plot of this story.**

_____

_____

_____

_____

5 **Imagine that Lupe loses to the girl in the baseball cap. Write a new outcome for this story.**

_____

_____

_____

_____

Tennessee

Reading Objective: Apply a variety of reading strategies.
Writing Objective: Write frequently for a variety of purposes such as narration, description, and personal creative expression.

Name _____

Text Structure

Text structure is the way a piece of writing is organized. Fiction can be organized with events in time order. Nonfiction can be organized in time order, by main idea with supporting details, by cause and effect, by compare and contrast, or by steps in a process. Notice how a written work is organized and whether special type or captions are given to help you understand.

Plants have many ways to spread pollen. Some flowers and trees offer an interesting contrast. The **bee orchid flower** looks and smells like a female bee. Male bees come to mate with the flower, but they end up spreading its pollen. The **carrion flower,** like the bee orchid, attracts insects by its odor. However, this flower smells like rotten meat and attracts flies that pollinate the flower. On the other hand, not all plants need to attract other living creatures to spread their pollen. **Oak and birch trees** use the wind to carry their pollen.

1 Which choice best describes this selection?

A fiction

B nonfiction

C both fiction and nonfiction

D neither fiction nor nonfiction

2 Which choice best describes how this selection is organized?

F time order

G reverse time order

H cause and effect

J compare and contrast

3 Which answer best completes the empty box shown below?

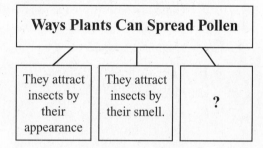

Ways Plants Can Spread Pollen		
They attract insects by their appearance	They attract insects by their smell.	?

A The flowers spread pollen.

B They don't need to spread pollen.

C The flowers have tiny wings.

D The wind spreads the pollen.

4 Why did the author use dark type for some of the words?

_____

_____

_____

_____

_____

_____

_____

Tennessee

Reading Objective: Apply a variety of reading strategies.
Writing Objective: Use appropriate organizational strategies to develop writing, including main idea and supporting details.

Name

Text Structure

Read "From Bees to Honey" (pages 285–297). Then answer the questions below.

1 Which choice best describes the selection?

A fiction

B nonfiction

C poetry

D drama

2 Which choice does <u>not</u> show that this selection is told in chronological order?

F John's work really doesn't start until April.

G John and Mary Ann don't make their living keeping bees.

H Early July is the peak of honey season in southwestern Minnesota.

J John wraps the hives in autumn.

3 How does the text structure of this story help the reader understand the content?

A by comparing the ways bees live with the ways humans live

B by telling you how to start your own hive

C by describing the yearly cycle of the bees and beekeeper

D by including photographs of young worker bees

4 Read page 290. All of the following are part of John's spring check except

F looking for brood eggs

G feeding hungry bees with sugar syrup

H recording the condition of each hive

J cleaning the bottles for honey

5 Suppose you spent one year living as a beekeeper. Write a list of the main events you would experience during the year. Be sure the events are in order.

_____

_____

_____

_____

_____

_____

_____

_____

_____

Tennessee

Reading Objective: Apply a variety of reading strategies.
Writing Objective: Use appropriate organizational strategies to develop writing, including main idea and supporting details.

Name _____

Text Structure

Read "From Bees to Honey" (pages 285–297). Then answer the questions below.

1 Which choice best describes how the selection is organized?

A as events in chronological order

B as a main idea with supporting details

C as a series of causes and effects

D as a demonstration of compare and contrast

2 Read the first two paragraphs on page 288. All of the following suggest chronological order except

F activities determined by the seasons

G cold winter as a quiet time

H a colony of bees

J beekeeper's year begins

3 Read the section "In the Honey House" (pages 295–296). How is the information organized?

A comparing and contrasting

B cause and effect

C steps in a process

D flashbacks

4 Use the description on page 288 and the picture on page 294 to explain how a bee suit protects the beekeeper from getting stung. Describe the suit from top to bottom.

_____

_____

_____

_____

5 If you were going to write a report on how a beekeeper collects honey, what text structure would you use? Explain why.

_____

_____

_____

_____

Reading Objective: Use comprehension strategies to enhance understanding, to make predictions, and to respond to literature.

Writing Objective: Use elements of the writing process as appropriate to the writing task.

Name _____

Summarizing

A summary is a brief telling of the main idea of an article or plot of a story. When a test asks you to give a summary or choose the best summary, go for the big idea, not specific details.

Dogs use many different sounds to tell what they want or how they feel. An excited dog might bark over and over again to show its joy. A contented dog sometimes makes a soft rumbling noise that sounds like a cat purring. A surprised dog often yelps, or gives a quick, high, loud scream. An angry dog might make a deep growl. Next time you hear these sounds and signals, think about what the dog might be "saying" to people and other animals.

1 **Which choice best summarizes this selection?**

A Dogs make many sounds to show how they feel.

B Happy dogs purr like cats.

C Smarter dogs make more sounds.

D Dogs can learn to speak English if you take time to teach them.

2 **A good title for the selection would be**

F Dogs Can Purr

G The Games Dogs Play

H Dog Sounds

J Dogs and Cats

3 **Which answer best completes the empty box shown below?**

Details	Summary
1. Dogs purr when they are happy. 2. Angry dogs growl. 3. Surprised dogs may yelp.	?

A Dogs know many words.

B Every dog is different.

C Dogs act strange when they are excited.

D Dogs make sounds to show their feelings.

4 **Which sentence in the article gives the best summary? Use the definition of *summary* at the beginning of this lesson to explain your chosen sentence.**

_____

_____

_____

_____

_____

_____

_____

Reading Objective: Use comprehension strategies to enhance understanding, to make predictions, and to respond to literature.
Writing Objective: Use elements of the writing process as appropriate to the writing task.

Tennessee

Name

Summarizing

Read "Babe to the Rescue" (pages 303–318). Then answer the questions below.

1 All of the following words describe Babe except

A friendly

B polite

C rude

D curious

2 Which sentence from the story best summarizes how Fly feels about ducks?

F "Now cuddle up, dear, and go to sleep."

G "Pigs are intelligent too."

H "Leave the silly things alone, they're not worth upsetting yourself about."

J "Was it a nasty dream?"

3 Which choice summarizes what happens on page 317?

A Ma dials 999 and talks for a long time.

B Babe squeals with fright and fury.

C The animals make noise to alert Mrs. Hogget.

D Babe ruins the rustlers' raid and saves the sheep.

4 Which word summarizes Mrs. Hogget's final feelings toward Babe?

F protective

G jealous

H curious

J furious

5 Read "The Hero Ham" (page 321). Summarize the ways that Babe and Priscilla are alike.

_____

_____

_____

_____

_____

_____

_____

_____

_____

_____

Tennessee

Reading Objective: Use comprehension strategies to enhance understanding, to make predictions, and to respond to literature.
Writing Objective: Use elements of the writing process as appropriate to the writing task.

Name _____

Summarizing

Read "The Hero Ham" (page 321). Then answer the questions below.

1 Which is the best summary of this story?

   A Ms. Herberta, her son, and friends spend the day at Lake Somerville.

   B All pigs are heroes.

   C Priscilla the pig becomes a hero when she saves a drowning boy.

   D Pigs can make great pets because they swim and wear nail polish.

2 Another good title for this story could be

   F Piggy Paddle to the Rescue

   G Welcome to the Pet Hall of Fame

   H A True Story

   J A Trip to the Lake

3 Read the second paragraph. Which of the following is the best summary?

   A Pigs are messy and funny looking.

   B Pigs have a bad reputation.

   C Messy rooms are often called pigsties.

   D People make fun of pigs' round shape.

4 Read "Babe to the Rescue" (pages 303–318). Who do you think is the better hero, Babe or Priscilla? Present an award to the pig of your choice that summarizes its heroic deeds.

_____

_____

_____

_____

5 Imagine you have to write a short article about Priscilla for a newspaper. Write a catchy title and a few sentences that tell about Priscilla.

_____

_____

_____

_____

_____

_____

Tennessee

Reading Objective: Improve comprehension by interpreting, analyzing, synthesizing, and evaluating written text.
Writing Objective: Write to acquire knowledge and clarify thinking.

Name _____

Compare and Contrast

Comparing means telling how two or more things are alike. Contrasting is telling how things are different. Test questions that use clue words such as *similar to, like, as, different from, but*, or *unlike* may be asking you to compare or contrast.

This year, my tenth birthday party was much more fun than my ninth birthday party last year. Last year, we stayed at my house and a clown came to entertain us. This year, we went to a bowling alley and took over six lanes. I had ten friends at the party this year, but last year just my relatives came over. The food this year was better too because we had pizza and cake instead of just cupcakes. I wonder what my eleventh birthday will be like?

1 How were the two parties described in the selection alike?

A One was better than the other was.

B Each was a bowling party.

C They were birthday parties.

D They each had pizza.

2 Which choice best describes how the birthdays were different?

F One birthday had better food than the other did.

G The tenth birthday was more fun.

H The narrator thinks that pizza tastes better than cupcakes.

J There were more people at the tenth birthday.

3 Which answer best completes the chart below?

Ninth Birthday Party	Tenth Birthday Party
1. at home	1. at a bowling alley
2. relatives came	2. friends came
3. cupcakes	3. ?

A pizza and cake

B six lanes at the bowling alley

C much more fun than last year

D no clowns

4 Compare and contrast the two parties. Name at least one way they were alike and one way they were different.

_____

_____

_____

_____

_____

Reading Objective: Improve comprehension by interpreting, analyzing, synthesizing, and evaluating written text.
Writing Objective: Write to acquire knowledge and clarify thinking.

Tennessee

Name _____

Compare and Contrast

Read "The Yangs' First Thanksgiving" (pages 331–346). Then answer the questions below.

1 Which of the following statements best describes how people in China feel about growing old?

A They are glad that they do not have to work.

B It is a shame.

C It is better to be young and served first at the table.

D It is an honor.

2 What do Holly and the narrator have in common?

F They come from China.

G They both play the viola.

H They play in the orchestra together.

J They have the same mother.

3 How are the narrator and her mother alike?

A Both think Mrs. Hanson acts strangely.

B Both want to impress Holly Hanson.

C Both are comfortable with American customs.

D Neither one wants to have dinner with the Conners.

4 Which choice best summarizes the differences between the Yangs and the Hansons?

F They come from different cultures.

G The Yangs are funnier than the Hansons.

H The Yangs have all boys.

J The Hansons and the Yangs like music.

5 Compare and contrast Mrs. Hanson and Mrs. Yang. Give at least two examples of how they are alike and two examples of how they are different.

_____

_____

_____

_____

_____

_____

_____

_____

_____

_____

Tennessee

Reading Objective: Improve comprehension by interpreting, analyzing, synthesizing, and evaluating written text.
Writing Objective: Write to acquire knowledge and clarify thinking.

Name _____

Compare and Contrast

Read "The Yangs' First Thanksgiving" (pages 331–346). Then answer the questions below.

1 **Which of the following best compares Holly and the narrator?**

  A They both come from China.

  B They both have pets.

  C They both play in the orchestra.

  D They both have brothers and sisters.

2 **What belief is widely held in China but not in America?**

  F It is an honor to grow older.

  G All families should have a pet.

  H Young people should be served food first.

  J It is very important to be thin.

3 **All of the following statements about the Yangs and Hansons are true except**

  A the Hansons enjoy Thanksgiving but the Yangs do not

  B the Yangs have a larger family than the Hansons

  C the Hansons and the Yangs have different feelings about getting old

  D the Hansons were born in America, and the Yangs are from China

4 **Compare and contrast the narrator and Holly. Give at least two examples of how they are alike and two examples of how they are different.**

_____

_____

_____

_____

_____

5 **Read the author's biography on page 347. How is Ms. Namioka similar to the narrator in her story? Give at least two examples.**

_____

_____

_____

_____

© Scott Foresman 5

Tennessee

Reading Objective: Apply a variety of reading strategies.
Writing Objective: Use appropriate organizational strategies to develop writing, including main ideas and supporting details.

Name _____

Main Idea and Supporting Details

The main idea is the most important idea about a topic. The supporting details tell more about the main idea. Test questions that ask what a piece of writing is mostly about are asking for the main idea.

What does a musher look for in a sled dog? First, most sled dogs are a type of dog known as the Alaskan husky, which are mixed-breed dogs, or mutts. People who breed huskies are looking for dogs with a strong instinct for pulling. Although sled dogs are strong enough to pull hundreds of pounds, they are not very large. The best sled dogs can weigh less than 55 pounds. One Iditarod musher had a dog that weighed just 43 pounds but could pull over 800 pounds. Some people think smaller dogs are stronger and faster than larger dogs. It's easier for oxygen and blood to travel to their hearts, lungs, and muscles. Once a dog with potential is found, it has to be trained. Mushers work for months teaching dogs to work together as a team. They even train when there is no snow on the ground. To do this, some mushers rope their dog teams to wheeled carts and let the dogs pull the carts over dirt roads. It takes time and effort to train a good sled dog. But once a dog is trained, it can work for years.

1 This passage is mostly about

A what makes a good sled dog

B the size of the best sled dogs

C mushers

D how to train sled dogs without snow

2 Which choice would be the best title for this selection?

F Sled Dogs That Compete in Races

G What a Sled Dog Looks Like

H How to Pick a Good Sled Dog

J The Alaskan Husky

3 Which answer best completes the chart below?

Main Idea: Sled dogs are not very large.

Supporting Details

"The best sled dogs can weigh less than 55 pounds."	**?**	"It's easier for oxygen and blood to travel to their hearts, lungs, and muscles."

A "But once a dog is trained, it can work for years."

B "It takes time and effort to train a good sled dog."

C "Once a dog with potential is found, it has to be trained."

D "One Iditarod musher had a dog that weighed just 43 pounds but could pull over 800 pounds."

4 Which sentence in the paragraph states the main idea? Give details to support your choice.

_____

_____

_____

Reading Objective: Apply a variety of reading strategies.
Writing Objective: Use appropriate organizational strategies to develop writing, including main ideas and supporting details.

Tennessee

Name _____

Main Idea and Supporting Details

Read "The Jr. Iditarod Race" (pages 355–368). Then answer the questions below.

1 The introduction on pages 356–357 is mainly about

A Alaskan winters

B diphtheria in Nome in 1925

C how the Iditarod and the Jr. Iditarod began

D the meaning of the word *Iditarod*

2 Read the last paragraph on page 363. Which sentence best expresses the main idea?

F the first

G the fourth

H the fifth

J the last

3 Which detail from the text best supports the idea that huskies love to race?

A "QT and Blacky have splits in the webs between their toes."

B "The dogs are pulling so hard now that five people can barely hold them back."

C "It's zero degrees, which is perfect for the dogs."

D "They cross the lake safely, following the red plastic cones marking the route."

4 Based on the details of the early part of the race, what can you conclude about Dusty?

F He does not realize that mushing is a dangerous sport.

G He has not prepared well for the race.

H He panics at the first sign of trouble.

J He makes intelligent decisions.

5 What is the main idea of the second paragraph on page 364? State it in your own words and provide supporting details.

_____

_____

_____

_____

_____

_____

© Scott Foresman 5

Tennessee

Reading Objective: Apply a variety of reading strategies.
Writing Objective: Use appropriate organizational strategies to develop writing, including main ideas and supporting details.

Name _____

Main Idea and Supporting Details

Read "The Jr. Iditarod Race" (pages 355–368). Then answer the questions below.

1 Which choice best states what the introduction on pages 356–357 is mainly about?

A the difficult winters in Alaska

B how medicine stopped diphtheria in Nome in 1925

C how the Iditarod and the Jr. Iditarod came about

D the dangers of the Iditarod

2 Read the second paragraph on page 368. What choice best states the main idea?

F The dogs are jumping and barking.

G Dusty's dogs were the fastest team.

H The dogs are champions.

J Rumors that the dogs were mistreated were shown to be untrue.

3 All of the following are dangers for mushers except

A moose

B snowmobiles

C zero-degree temperatures

D collisions

4 Read page 364. Write the main idea and then list at least three supporting details.

_____

_____

_____

_____

5 Write a new title for this story. Explain why you think that title expresses the main idea of the story.

_____

_____

_____

_____

Name _____

Predicting

Predicting is figuring out what you think will happen next in a story. Test questions may ask you to predict what will happen late in a story. Base your prediction on what you know from the story already and on common sense.

Charlie and Stacy had been planning all week to sleep in a tent in their backyard on Friday night. Unfortunately, the weather was very bad. Their mother had suggested that they camp out another night, but they set up the tent anyway. The wind was howling. It whipped the sides of the tent and blew in through the door flaps. The pieces of their game of checkers skated off the board and scattered all over the sleeping bags. The temperature was dropping, and by 9 o'clock the thermometer read 49 degrees. At 10:30, rain started to make pit-a-pat noises on the nylon roof. Although the material was advertised as waterproof, Stacy could feel some moisture seeping through. It was not a good night for backyard camping.

1 **What do you think will most likely happen to Charlie and Stacy?**

A They will have a warm, dry night in the tent.

B They will have to go back to the house during the night.

C Their mother will join them in the tent.

D The weather will get better.

2 **Anything left inside the tent will probably**

F stay warm

G get wet

H stay the same

J stay dry

3 **Which answer best completes the chart below?**

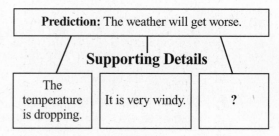

A It is Friday night.

B The tent blows over.

C It is starting to rain.

D Charlie and Stacy have bad luck.

4 **Write two or three sentences that describe what you think will happen the next time Charlie and Stacy plan to camp outside.**

_____

_____

_____

_____

© Scott Foresman 5

Reading Objective: Use comprehension strategies to enhance understanding, to make predictions, and to respond to literature.
Writing Objective: Continue to respond actively and imaginatively to literature.

Tennessee

Name

Predicting

Read "The Night Alone" (pages 373–386). Then answer the questions below.

1 Read page 384. Which of the following is a clue that Ohkwa'ri will see a rattlesnake?

A "I'm a hungry, hungry bear."

B "Suddenly he heard a sound like pebbles being shaken in a hollow gourd."

C "His thoughts were divided between his hunger and his memory of Grabber's story."

D "He began to walk faster as he thought of food."

2 When the story says that Ohkwa'ri "was no longer watching where he put his feet," you can predict that

F he will return to the longhouse

G he will step into a dangerous situation

H he will continue to feel hungry

J he will need to find shoes

3 Which is <u>not</u> a logical prediction you could make based on the picture and the first paragraph on page 383?

A Walks with the Bears will proudly show the cub to the village.

B The mother bear will become angry.

C Walks with the Bears will be injured.

D Walks with the Bears will not steal the cub.

4 Based on what happens in the story, what do you think will probably happen after Ohkwa'ri has his morning meal on page 386?

F He will continue his adventures.

G He will return immediately to his family at the longhouse.

H He will be killed by a rattlesnake.

J He will ask his sister's help to find food.

5 Predict how Ohkwa'ri will be different when he returns to the longhouse after his adventures end.

_____

_____

_____

_____

_____

_____

_____

_____

Tennessee

Reading Objective: Use comprehension strategies to enhance understanding, to make predictions, and to respond to literature.
Writing Objective: Continue to respond actively and imaginatively to literature.

Name _____

Predicting

Read "The Night Alone" (pages 373–386). Then answer the questions below.

1 Which of the following is the best clue that Ohkwa'ri will make it through the night alone?

A "He could hear his own breathing."

B "The next time he woke was when he heard a strange sound."

C "'Wherever I go, I will never be truly alone.'"

D "'I will not wake again,' he said to himself after that second time. But he was wrong."

2 Read the paragraph that starts on page 381 and continues on page 382. What detail helps you predict that Grabber's tattoo will <u>not</u> turn out right?

F Most people had tattoos.

G Grabber was not a good artist.

H He wanted people to call him Walks with the Bears.

J He was nicknamed "Grabber."

3 If you were to extend the story beyond the ending here, Ohkwa'ri would most likely

A continue his adventures

B return immediately to his family at the longhouse

C be killed by a rattlesnake

D need his sister's help to find food

4 Imagine that Ohkwa'ri comes home and tells his father what happened during his time away from the longhouse. What do you predict he will say?

_____

_____

_____

5 Read "How the Sun Came" (pages 389–391). How is this tale similar to the story Ohkwa'ri tells about Grabber?

_____

_____

_____

© Scott Foresman 5

Reading Objective: Extend reading vocabulary utilizing context.
Writing Objective: Demonstrate effective writing style by the use of vivid words, varied sentences, and appropriate transitions.

Tennessee

Name _____

Context Clues

Context clues are words near an unfamiliar word that help you understand it. If a test question asks about a word you do not know, you may be able to figure out its meaning from words nearby.

Marion Jones, the track and field superstar, burst onto the international track scene in 1997. She captured that season's best times in the 100-meter and 200-meter races and the American-best long jump. She became famous in many countries. She also received many accolades, such as the Jesse Owens International Trophy Award. This award honors the best athlete of the year. After 1997, her debut year, Jones's career has continued to skyrocket. Jones has brought attention back to track and field in the United States. She has become the first American woman to be ranked number one in three different events simultaneously. At the same time, she was first in the 100-meter, the 200-meter, and the long jump. She breaks stadium records routinely and has even broken her own records regularly. Marion Jones wins the races she enters as a matter of habit!

1 The passage says, "She also received many accolades, such as the Jesse Owens International Trophy Award." What does the word *accolades* mean?

A songs

B awards

C letters

D defeats

2 The passage says, "After 1997, her debut year, Jones's career has continued to skyrocket." The word *debut* means

F second

G last

H first

J final

3 Which phrase best completes the chart below?

Word	routinely
Definition	on a regular basis
Context Clues	1. regularly 2. ?

A as a matter of habit

B skyrocket

C famous

D enters

4 Find the word *simultaneously* in the passage. Tell what the word means, and which context clues helped you decide. Then use *simultaneously* in a sentence of your own.

_____

_____

_____

_____

Tennessee

Reading Objective: Extend reading vocabulary utilizing context.
Writing Objective: Demonstrate effective writing style by the use of vivid words, varied sentences, and appropriate transitions.

Name _____

Context Clues

Read "The Heart of a Runner" (pages 395–414). Then answer the questions below.

1 What words and phrases on page 397 give the most useful clues about the meaning of *sprain*?

A jump up, stop moving

B buzzing around in my head

C ankle twisted, not broken

D track meet

2 What does the word *rabbit* mean as it is used in this story?

F a track coach

G someone who runs barelegged

H a person who helps pace another runner

J a small animal that runs fast

3 A sentence in the story says that a name will "be inscribed on the brass plate." What choice best describes what will happen to the name?

A It will be written on the plate.

B The team will change their name.

C Ebonee will carry it.

D It will be erased from the plate.

4 On page 416, Ms. Mathis says that she imagined Ebonee as "a kind of human encyclopedia, a living database." This description refers to Ebonee's

F speed

G knowledge

H pacer

J trophy

5 Read "Rituals for Winning" (pages 419–421). Define *superstition* in your own words. Give an example of a superstition held by Ebonee Rose and one held by a professional athlete from the article.

_____

_____

_____

_____

_____

_____

_____

_____

_____

© Scott Foresman 5

Name _____

Context Clues

Read "The Heart of a Runner" (pages 395–414). Then answer the questions below.

1 What does the word *anchor* mean, as it is used on page 402?

A something heavy that holds a boat in place

B a very heavy person

C the last runner on a relay team

D the first runner on a relay team

2 Before the race, Ebonee says that the "petals within me began to flutter." The best synonym for *flutter* is

F run very fast

G fall down

H scare

J tremble

3 Read the second paragraph on page 403. What is the meaning of the word *overcome* as it is used here?

A strongly affected by emotion

B defeat a problem

C remain helpless

D make a mistake

4 Use information provided on page 402 to explain why the anchor runner has such an important job.

_____

_____

_____

_____

5 Read the article "Rituals of Winning" (pages 419–421). Use context clues to define *rituals* and explain how you figured out its meaning.

_____

_____

_____

_____

_____

Reading Objective: Read independently for a variety of purposes.
Writing Objective: Use appropriate organizational strategies to develop writing, including main ideas and supporting details.

Tennessee

Name _____

Author's Purpose

An author's purpose is the reason the author has for writing. It may be to inform, persuade, express, or entertain. Sometimes an author may have more than one purpose—for example, to entertain and inform.

RECIPE: Gram's Quick Spaghetti Sauce   serves 2
1. Cook the pasta.
2. Cook 1 tablespoon of olive oil and 2 cloves of chopped garlic over low heat for 2 minutes.
3. Add a 28 ounce can of whole tomatoes and mash them with a spoon.
4. Add 1 teaspoon of salt and a dash of sugar.
5. Cook on medium heat for 15 minutes.
6. Combine the sauce with the spaghetti and serve with grated cheese.

---

1 The main reason the author has written this paragraph is to

A persuade the reader that it is better to buy food in a can or jar

B show what a good cook he or she is

C inform the reader about an easy recipe for spaghetti sauce

D entertain hungry readers

2 Imagine the author of this recipe has written the following books. Which title does <u>not</u> seem intended to persuade?

F We Must Stop Eating Junk Food

G Learn Why You Should Become a Better Cook

H Everyone Can Lose Weight

J George Baskin's 101 Cookie Recipes

3 Which answer best completes the chart below?

```
┌─────────────────────────────────┐
│ Main Purpose: Show that home    │
│ cooking can be easy             │
└─────────────────────────────────┘

         Supporting Details:
┌──────────┐ ┌──────────┐ ┌──────────┐
│ show     │ │ use      │ │    ?     │
│ easy     │ │ everyday │ │          │
│ recipes  │ │ ingred.  │ │          │
└──────────┘ └──────────┘ └──────────┘
```

A use simple directions

B make recipes that serve only two people

C use family recipes

D cook only spaghetti recipes

4 In your own words, describe the author's purpose in writing this recipe card. Explain how the way the recipe card is written supports the author's purpose.

_____

_____

_____

Reading Objective: Read independently for a variety of purposes.
Writing Objective: Use appropriate organizational strategies to develop writing, including main ideas and supporting details.

Name _____

Author's Purpose

Read *The Memory Box* (pages 425–437). Then answer the questions below.

1 Why does the author describe the fishing trip in detail?

A to give the reader a chance to learn new vocabulary words about fishing

B to convince the reader that fishing is an excellent hobby

C to entertain the reader with funny stories

D to show the reader how the experience would be worth remembering

2 What is the best reason the author chose Zach to narrate the story?

F He can show what it is like to love someone who has Alzheimer's.

G He is the youngest person in the story.

H He owns the memory box.

J He has the best memory of all the characters in the story.

3 On page 434, Gram tells Zach that Gramps forgot his shoes. What does that statement mean to Zach?

A that Gram forgot to give Gramps his shoes

B that Gramps must be fishing

C that Zach should take off his shoes

D that something is wrong with Gramps

4 Gramps tells Zach, "No matter what happens to the old person, the memories are saved forever." This statement shows that

F he has made many memory boxes

G he is worried that something is wrong

H Zach is too young to understand

J Gram does not want him to make a memory box

5 What do you think was the author's main reason or reasons for writing *The Memory Box?* Support your answer with examples from the story.

_____

_____

_____

_____

_____

_____

_____

_____

Reading Objective: Read independently for a variety of purposes.
Writing Objective: Use appropriate organizational strategies to develop writing, including main ideas and supporting details.

Tennessee

Name _____

Author's Purpose

Read *The Memory Box* **(pages 425–437). Then answer the questions below.**

1 **Read pages 426–427. What is the author's purpose?**

A to establish that Zach and Gramps have a good relationship

B to show that Gramps is an excellent fisherman

C to inform the reader of the best way to catch fish

D to show that Gramps is not feeling like himself

2 **Read the last paragraph on page 428. What do you think is the reason the author includes it?**

F to persuade

G to excite

H to entertain

J to inform

3 **All of the following details show Gramps is forgetful except**

A he goes out without his shoes

B he walks in the poison ivy

C he doesn't shave

D he describes how to clean fish

4 **How does reading** *The Memory Box* **make you feel? Explain how the author's writing made you feel this way.**

_____

_____

_____

5 **Write a paragraph that would convince your family to start a memory box. Use details and language that will persuade your reader.**

_____

_____

_____

_____

Reading Objective: Experience and develop interest in literature which includes gender diversity.
Writing Objective: Write frequently for a variety of purposes such as narration, description, and personal, creative expression.

Tennessee

Name _____

Setting

The setting of a story is its time and place. When you answer test questions that ask about the setting of a story, identify the time and place and consider how they affect the characters and events.

On June 4, 1919, the U.S. Congress voted to add the Nineteenth Amendment to the Constitution. The amendment, which would give women the right to vote, needed approval by thirty-six states. By August of 1920, thirty-five states had passed it. It was then that the final vote came to Nashville, Tennessee. Women's suffrage celebrities from Boston, New York, and Chicago arrived in Nashville to help push the bill through. They were united under a single symbol: the yellow rose. Anti-Suffragists wore red roses. On the day of the vote, the Suffragists could see they were in trouble. After two roll calls, the vote was tied. Then the legislators had a third roll call. Wearing a red rose, Representative Harry Burn broke the deadlock by voting in favor of the bill. The Anti-Suffragists began chasing Burn. To escape the angry mob, Burn climbed out a third-floor window of the Capitol. Making his way along a ledge, he was able to save himself by hiding in the Capitol attic. Later, Burn was asked to explain the red rose on his jacket. He said that he had received a telegram from his mother in East Tennessee, urging him to vote in favor of the amendment. On August 26, 1920, the Nineteenth Amendment became national law.

1 **Where does this story take place?**

A Nashville, Tennessee

B East Tennessee

C Boston

D Philadelphia

2 **When does this story take place?**

F June 4, 1991

G August, 1820

H June, 1920

J August, 1920

3 **Where does the vote take place?**

A East Tennessee

B the Capitol Building

C the Capitol attic

D Chicago

4 **How does the setting of this story affect the actions of the characters? Use examples from the story to explain your answer.**

_____

_____

_____

_____

_____

Tennessee

Reading Objective: Experience and develop interest in literature which includes gender diversity.
Writing Objective: Write frequently for a variety of purposes such as narration, description, and personal, creative expression.

Name _____

Setting

Read "I Want to Vote!" (pages 449–463). Then answer the questions below.

1 When does this story take place?

A during the American Revolution

B during the Civil War

C in the early 1900s

D during World War II

2 At the beginning of the story, Lila sells newspapers on the street. What is unusual about this setting?

F The street is full of women holding a parade.

G The street is empty.

H She is the only girl on the street.

J She is the only girl selling newspapers.

3 During the time the story takes place, what is one thing women are <u>not</u> allowed to do?

A hold a parade

B vote in an election

C read newspapers

D talk to their fathers

4 All of the choices give clues about the story's setting except

F a parade from Washington Square to Fifty-ninth Street

G flames forty feet high

H the corner of Tenth Street

J 1917 in America

5 Judging from the pictures alone in this story, what could you determine about the general time and place of this story?

_____

_____

_____

_____

_____

_____

_____

_____

_____

_____

Tennessee

Reading Objective: Experience and develop interest in literature which includes gender diversity.
Writing Objective: Write frequently for a variety of purposes such as narration, description, and personal, creative expression.

Name _____

Setting

Read "I Want to Vote!" (pages 449–463). Then answer the questions below.

1 **Which of the following does _not_ tell you about the setting?**

- **A** Lila lives in New York City.
- **B** Lila and Grandmama march up Fifth Avenue.
- **C** Lila convinces Papa to let her march in the parade.
- **D** This story takes place in the early 1900s.

2 **Which of the following does _not_ let you know that this story takes place in the past?**

- **F** Women cannot vote.
- **G** Lila wants to sell newspapers.
- **H** Mike wears knickers.
- **J** Lila rides on a trolley.

3 **How is the setting at the end of the story like the setting at the beginning?**

- **A** Lila stands in a crowd of many women.
- **B** This story takes place in the early 1900s.
- **C** It is twilight.
- **D** Lila is not standing in a crowd of newsboys.

4 **The story never actually states in which city Lila lives. Use clues in the story to decide which city is the setting.**

_____

_____

_____

_____

5 **The setting of this story strongly affects the events in Lila's life. What might Lila be fighting for if the story took place today?**

_____

_____

_____

_____

© Scott Foresman 5

Reading Objective: Improve comprehension by interpreting, analyzing, synthesizing, and evaluating written text.
Writing Objective: Write frequently for a variety of purposes.

Tennessee

Name _____

Paraphrasing

Paraphrasing is explaining something in your own words. If you are asked to paraphrase a written work on a test, use your own words but don't add your opinion or change the author's meaning.

Frederick Douglass was born a slave in 1817. As he grew up, he knew that he wanted to be free. At the age of 21, he escaped from his master and went north in search of freedom. He finally reached Massachusetts, where he lived as a free man. Douglass helped runaway slaves escape to freedom. When the Civil War began, he organized black soldiers for the Union army. After the war, he continued to work for equal treatment and voting rights for blacks. He described his fight for freedom and justice in *Narrative of the Life of Frederick Douglass*. Today he is remembered as a powerful speaker and a hero who fought for justice.

1 **Which choice best paraphrases the first four sentences?**

A Douglass was a slave who longed for freedom.

B Douglass lived in Massachusetts as a slave.

C Douglass fought hard to obtain the freedom of other slaves.

D Born a slave, Douglass escaped at 21 to freedom in Massachusetts.

2 **Which choice best paraphrases what Douglass did as a free man?**

F He fought for the freedom and equality of slaves and wrote a book.

G He died while escaping to the north.

H All by himself, he ended slavery and became a hero and a writer.

J He lived as a slave in Massachusetts, where he married.

3 **Which answer best completes the empty box shown below?**

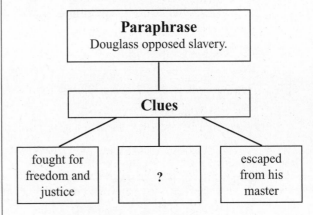

A born a slave in 1817

B helped runaway slaves

C is a hero

D is remembered today

4 **Paraphrase the selection.**

_____

_____

_____

_____

Reading Objective: Improve comprehension by interpreting, analyzing, synthesizing, and evaluating written text.
Writing Objective: Write frequently for a variety of purposes.

Tennessee

Name _____

Paraphrasing

Read "The Long Path to Freedom" (pages 469–484). Then answer the questions below.

1 Which choice best paraphrases the first two paragraphs of the story?

A Harriet discovers that she has been tricked but does not want to be free because her mother is still a slave.

B Rit's owner frees Harriet from slavery in his will.

C Another owner has snatched Harriet, which is an unfair thing to do to a freed slave.

D Harriet realizes she must gain freedom for herself after learning that her own mother had been tricked out of freedom.

2 Read pages 476–477. Which choice best paraphrases Harriet's relationship with the Quaker woman?

F The Quaker woman lets Harriet live with her in freedom.

G The Quaker woman takes Harriet's quilt and returns her to Dr. Thompson.

H Harriet helps the Quaker woman escape to freedom.

J The Quaker woman helps Harriet escape to freedom.

3 Read the last two paragraphs on page 478. Which choice best paraphrases these paragraphs?

A Harriet is too tired to walk anymore, so she has a sleeping spell.

B Harriet has a sleeping spell as she walks along the road and wakes up when she hears slave hunters.

C Harriet is afraid she will fall asleep if she moves.

D Harriet is brave enough to talk to the men when she awakes after her sleeping spell.

4 At the end of the story, Harriet reflects on her experience being free. A paraphrase of the final paragraph on page 484 should include all of the following choices except

F she was free after a dangerous journey

G she would never return to Maryland

H she would lead her family to freedom

J she felt like a stranger

5 In the middle of page 481, Harriet sees a man in a graveyard. Paraphrase this experience and explain what happened.

_____

_____

_____

_____

_____

Tennessee

Reading Objective: Improve comprehension by interpreting, analyzing, synthesizing, and evaluating written text.
Writing Objective: Write frequently for a variety of purposes.

Name _____

Paraphrasing

Read "The Long Path to Freedom" (pages 469–484). Then answer the questions below.

1 Read page 475. Which choice best paraphrases this section?

 A Harriet sings a song.

 B Harriet and Mary chat in the kitchen about the best ways to escape.

 C Harriet tells Mary that she should run away with her.

 D Harriet sings a goodbye song to Mary.

2 On page 474, Harriet says, "There's one of two things I've got a right to, liberty or death." What does Harriet mean?

 F If I am caught, then I will die.

 G I prefer death to slavery.

 H In Pennsylvania I will be free.

 J My family has a right to be free.

3 Harriet is free at the end of the story. Select the best paraphrase of her feelings.

 A She is sorry that she has escaped.

 B She still wants to help free her family.

 C She wants to return to her husband.

 D She is angry that no one welcomes her to freedom.

4 Paraphrase Harriet's experience with Mr. Garrett, as described on page 482.

_____

_____

_____

_____

5 Read the article "How the Underground Railroad Got Its Name" (pages 487–489). Paraphrase this article.

_____

_____

_____

_____

_____

© Scott Foresman 5

Tennessee

Reading Objective: Apply a variety of reading strategies.
Writing Objective: Continue to respond actively and imaginatively to literature.

Name _____

Visualizing

Visualizing is making a picture in your mind as you read. Authors can help you visualize by using imagery and describing how things look, smell, sound, taste, or feel. On a test you may be asked to identify ways an author helps you visualize things in a story.

All of a sudden Fluffy's airplane grew to a gigantic size. Fluffy and Whiskers flopped down into the huge seats. The paper airplane took off! They soared through the warm air, and the wind flattened their whiskers against their fuzzy faces. Fluffy and Whiskers loved flying over the city streets. They didn't even mind the fact that they were only about one inch tall each. At last, the paper airplane landed in a warm, gooey puddle of melted pink strawberry ice cream. Fluffy took a deep breath. What an adventure!

1 Based on the descriptions in the selection, what does the word *gigantic* most likely mean?

A smooth

B large

C small

D humid

2 The weather during Fluffy and Whiskers's ride is

F cold and snowy

G hot and rainy

H cool and cloudy

J warm and breezy

3 Which answer best completes the web shown below?

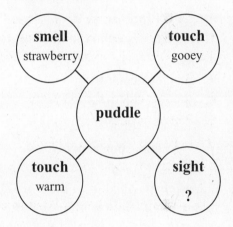

A sweet

B delicious

C hot

D pink

4 Describe what it will probably feel like for Fluffy and Whiskers when they get off the airplane. Explain which words in the story help you create that description.

_____

_____

_____

_____

Reading Objective: Apply a variety of reading strategies.
Writing Objective: Continue to respond actively and imaginatively to literature.

Tennessee

Name _____

Visualizing

Read *from Chester Cricket's Pigeon Ride* (pages 493–511). Then answer the questions below.

1 How does Lulu's speech make her sound most like a pigeon?

A She uses large words.

B She repeats the sound at the end of words like "you" as if she were cooing.

C She tells funny stories.

D She cannot speak because she is a bird, so she just chirps.

2 In paragraph two on page 502, Chester hears all of the following except

F a pigeon cooing

G a brook splashing

H the shooshing of leaves

J insect and animal noises

3 Based on the description on page 502, which choice best describes how Chester feels when they land in Central Park?

A tired

B silly

C excited

D angry

4 Which of the following phrases from the story does not help the reader visualize Chester and Lulu's ride?

F "jiggling reflection of the moon"

G "tree-smelling night"

H "whispering of insects"

J "approached their final destination"

5 Choose a passage from the story that you can visualize. Describe what you see in your mind and explain which words in the story help you visualize the scene. Remember that you can visualize with all your senses, not just sight.

_____

_____

_____

_____

_____

_____

_____

_____

Tennessee

Reading Objective: Apply a variety of reading strategies.
Writing Objective: Continue to respond actively and imaginatively to literature.

Name _____

Visualizing

Read *from Chester Cricket's Pigeon Ride* (pages 493–511). Then answer the questions below.

1 All of these phrases from the story help you visualize the city except

A "ready for another adventure"

B "dome of light glowing over it"

C "taxis, all jittered along like miniatures"

D "skyscrapers rise up like a grove of steel trees"

2 Which choice does not help you visualize the lake in Central Park on page 502?

F a pigeon cooing

G a brook splashing

H the shooshing of leaves

J insect and animal noises

3 Which of the following best helps you visualize Chester and Lulu's flight?

A Chester and Lulu were flying high.

B Chester saw a famous building.

C There is a big lake in the city.

D New York City glowed and sparkled in the moonlight.

4 What do you think Chester is visualizing as he falls, according to the picture on page 507? Describe for readers the things he sees and hears.

_____

_____

_____

_____

5 Write a paragraph about an adventure in a boat, on a bus, or in a car. Include descriptions that will help the reader visualize the scene.

_____

_____

_____

_____

© Scott Foresman 5

Reading Objective: Develop skills in making inferences and recognizing unstated assumptions.
Writing Objective: Write frequently for a variety of purposes.

Tennessee

Name _____

Context Clues

Context clues are words that help you understand an unfamiliar word. If a test question asks about a word you do not know, look for other words in the story or article that might define or describe this word.

> The townspeople came together to commemorate the new war memorial. Hundreds of adults and children gathered at the site. The statue was covered with a large cloth. The crowd waited nearly 45 minutes, but eventually Mayor Drysdale walked up to the platform and removed the cloth. The town saw the statue unveiled for the first time. After a moment of silence, the crowd clapped their approval. Everyone agreed that this day would be remembered for decades.

1 The word *commemorate* most likely means

A honor

B ignore

C copy

D enjoy

2 Which phrase in the selection is the most helpful clue to the meaning of *eventually*?

F "gathered at the site"

G "covered with a large cloth"

H "waited nearly 45 minutes"

J "remembered for decades"

3 Which answer best completes the chart shown below?

Word	Definition	Context Clues
unveiled	revealed	• ___?___ • "removed the cloth" • "saw the statue" • "for the first time"

A "remembered for decades"

B "clapped their approval"

C "walked up to the platform"

D "statue was covered with a large cloth"

4 Choose a word from the paragraph that you do not know. Try to define it using context clues. Explain how the context clues helped you.

_____

_____

_____

_____

_____

_____

_____

_____

Reading Objective: Develop skills in making inferences and recognizing unstated assumptions.
Writing Objective: Write frequently for a variety of purposes.

Tennessee

Name _____

Context Clues

Read *Passage to Freedom* (pages 519–531). Then answer the questions below.

1 Read the first paragraph on page 521. What does the word *diplomat* mean?

A a foreigner who works in a downstairs office

B a person who lives in Lithuania

C a man or woman from Japan

D a person who manages relations between nations

2 Read the last paragraph on page 523. Use context clues to figure out the meaning of *issue* as it is used in this story.

F a copy of a newspaper

G a topic to be debated

H to officially give out

J to glow with light or sound

3 Page 528 tells about Mr. Sugihara's experience writing visas. Based on the passage, which choice best describes how he feels?

A unsure but angry

B tired but determined

C confused but happy

D cheerful but puzzled

4 In the afterword of the story we learn that Mr. Sugihara and his family were put in an *internment camp*. What word or phrase on page 531 gives the best clue to the meaning of *internment camp*?

F export company

G imprisoned

H family treasures

J monument

5 Read page 527. Define *embraced* in your own words. Explain which context clues helped you create this definition.

_____

_____

_____

_____

_____

_____

_____

_____

© Scott Foresman 5

Name _____

Context Clues

Read *Passage to Freedom* (pages 519–531). Then answer the questions below.

1 Read the second paragraph on page 523. What word refers to people who ran away from their homes to escape being killed?

A crowd

B soldiers

C Nazis

D refugees

2 Read the fifth paragraph on page 524. The phrase *sent by cable* most likely means

F to send by mail

G to put a message on the television

H to send by telegraph

J to send by e-mail

3 Read the third paragraph on page 525. What does the word *superiors* mean?

A Jewish refugees

B government officials in charge

C Japanese diplomats

D Auntie Setsuko

4 Choose a word from *Passage to Freedom* that you did not know before you read the story. Use context clues to define the word and explain how you figured out its meaning.

_____

_____

_____

_____

5 Why do you think Mr. Sugihara decided to help the refugees? Use clues from the story to support your answer.

_____

_____

_____

_____

_____

© Scott Foresman 5

Name _____

Paraphrasing

Paraphrasing is explaining something in your own words. If you are asked to paraphrase a written work on a test, use your own words but don't add your opinion or change the author's meaning.

"And they're off!" The 21st annual Grand Gallop had begun. The horses bolted from their stalls. Each one sped down the lane. Their legs were running hard and their manes were flying in the air. Around the first turn, the horses started breathing heavily, and a shiny film of sweat could be seen on their skin. The jockeys urged them on. Around the final turn, Tony's Surprise took the lead and reached the finish line first. Later, in the winner's circle, the horse wore a blanket of flowers in victory. Of course, how would this horse know that he had run the fastest race ever in the history of the Grand Gallop?

1 **Which choice would not be included in a paraphrase of this story?**

A Horses ran in the 21st Grand Gallop.

B Tony's Surprise was injured in the last lap of the race.

C Tony's Surprise won.

D Tony's Surprise ran the fastest Grand Gallop in its history.

2 **Which choice best describes what happens to Tony's Surprise?**

F He took the lead on the last turn and won the race.

G He led the race until the last turn and then lost.

H He gave his best effort but never led the race.

J He was unable to race and stayed in his stall.

3 **Which answer best completes the chart shown below?**

Original Sentence
"Of course, how could this horse know that he had run the fastest race ever in the history of the Grand Gallop?"

↓

Paraphrase
?

A How could the horse ever know how fast it had run in the race?

B Did the horse know it had run the fastest race?

C The fastest race at the Grand Gallop was over.

D The horse didn't know it, but he had run the fastest time ever recorded at the Grand Gallop.

4 **Paraphrase the selection.**

_____

_____

_____

_____

Tennessee

Reading Objective: Improve comprehension by interpreting, analyzing, synthesizing, and evaluating written text.
Writing Objective: Write frequently for a variety of purposes.

Name

Paraphrasing

Read *Paul Revere's Ride* (pages 537–549). Then answer the questions below.

1 Which choice best states Paul Revere's plan if the British army marches from the town?

A He will do nothing since he is British.

B He will hide in the church tower.

C He will wait for a sign and then ride his horse to alert the people.

D He will hang a lantern in the church tower to tell people what is happening.

2 On page 545, Revere is described as "impatient to mount and ride, booted and spurred with a heavy stride." Which choice best paraphrases how he is feeling?

F sad but excited to visit the church

G angry but calm about war

H tired but happy that he won't have to fight

J nervous but ready to spread the word

3 Which choice best summarizes how Revere spends his night in Middlesex?

A He rides from town to town warning the people about the British.

B He fights the British with his musket.

C He rides to Medford, and then returns to the church.

D He falls asleep next to his horse.

4 What is the best paraphrase of the first stanza on page 549?

F Revere will be remembered for his defiant act of warning the farmers.

G Revere knocked at doors and made an echoing sound.

H Revere rode quickly in order to reach every Middlesex farmer.

J The farmers fought bravely because they were warned.

5 Read the last stanza on page 548. Paraphrase the fighting that occurred between the British and the American revolutionaries after Revere's ride.

_____

_____

_____

_____

_____

_____

_____

_____

© Scott Foresman 5

Tennessee

Reading Objective: Improve comprehension by interpreting, analyzing, synthesizing, and evaluating written text.
Writing Objective: Write frequently for a variety of purposes.

Name _____

Paraphrasing

Read *Paul Revere's Ride* (pages 537–549). Then answer the questions below.

1 Read page 538. Which is the best paraphrase of the second and third paragraphs?

  A I'll be waiting for the British so I can help them fight the farmers.

  B The North Church tower is a good place to hang a signal light.

  C If the British come, signal me from the church tower so I can warn people.

  D The country folk will spread the alarm.

2 According to page 543, the friend does all of the following except

  F fires a shot

  G pauses to listen

  H climbs to the tower

  J feels a spell

3 On page 546, the poet writes, "The fate of a nation was riding that night." Which choice best paraphrases this line?

  A Without Paul Revere, the British would have won the war.

  B Without Paul Revere, the church tower would have been burned.

  C A person named Fate was riding a horse.

  D Americans should only ride horses at night.

4 Imagine that you are Paul Revere. Give a brief paraphrase of your famous ride, using information from the poem.

_____

_____

_____

_____

5 Rewrite the last stanza of the poem in your own words.

_____

_____

_____

_____

Name _____

Theme

The theme of a story is its underlying meaning or message. A theme can be a statement, lesson, or generalization. If you are asked on a test to identify a theme, ask yourself, "What is the main message of this story?"

One day a humble fisherman caught a dolphin. When he discovered that the dolphin was actually a prince under a spell, he freed it. That night the fisherman told his wife what had happened, and she became angry with him. She made him go back to the dolphin and demand that it give her a cottage in return for having its life saved. The fisherman went back to the dolphin and requested a cottage, which was granted immediately. Still the wife was not happy. She sent her husband back to ask for a castle, which was granted immediately. But she wanted more. She sent the fisherman back to ask the dolphin to make her king. Once she was made king, she wanted to be emperor. Still the wife wasn't satisfied. Finally, she wished to control the sun, moon, and stars. When the fisherman made this last request to the dolphin, it became angry. The sea trembled, and rain fell heavily. The dolphin commanded the fisherman to go home. His wife was waiting for him in their hut.

1 **The word that does <u>not</u> describe the fisherman's wife is**

   A greedy

   B unreasonable

   C generous

   D dissatisfied

2 **The fisherman ends up in his old hut because**

   F he hated the castle

   G he asked for too much from the dolphin

   H his wife wanted to stay there

   J it was closer to the sea

3 **Which answer best completes the chart?**

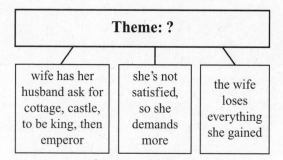

   A Never make dolphins angry at you.

   B Dolphins have special powers.

   C People who ask for too much can lose everything.

   D It's better to be a fisherman than a king.

4 **Suppose a younger person reads this story but does not understand the theme. What would you say to explain it to him or her?**

_____

_____

_____

Tennessee

Reading Objective: Improve comprehension by interpreting, analyzing, synthesizing, and evaluating written text.
Writing Objective: Continue to respond actively and imaginatively to literature.

Name _____

Theme

Read "The Baker's Neighbor" (pages 561–574). Then answer the questions below.

1 Which of the following is <u>not</u> important to Pablo?

A making money

B enjoying everyday pleasures

C being with friends

D smelling baked goods

2 Which sentence best states the theme of this play?

F Only the richest people can be happy.

G It is better to be a miser than be poor.

H The fastest way to be rich is to be a miser.

J Money alone cannot make a person happy.

3 All of the following support the answer to Question 2 except

A "Good friends and neighbors are better than gold!"

B "But it makes me happy to smell your pastries."

C "Are you going to count your money, Manuel?"

D "But I'd rather sit in the sun and take advantage of all the small, everyday pleasures that life has to offer."

4 According to this play, all of following are more important than money except

F friends

G family

H simple, everyday pleasures

J the cash box

5 Write a paragraph that continues the story after Manuel serves pastries. Show in this paragraph that he has changed.

_____

_____

_____

_____

_____

_____

_____

_____

_____

Tennessee

Reading Objective: Improve comprehension by interpreting, analyzing, synthesizing, and evaluating written text.
Writing Objective: Continue to respond actively and imaginatively to literature.

Name _____

Theme

Read "The Baker's Neighbor" (pages 561–574). Then answer the questions below.

1 Of the statements that the judge makes, which best states a theme of the play?

A "It gives you great pleasure to touch that gold, doesn't it, Manuel?"

B "In other words, he has smelled your pastry and you have touched his gold."

C "The fee I am asking is this—pies and cakes for everyone—free of charge!"

D "In the future, think less about making money and more about making friends."

2 Which of the following best states another theme of the play?

F It is good to work hard and make money.

G Some of the best things in life are free.

H Judges should always make good decisions.

J Children should share their food and money.

3 The detail in the final paragraph that indicates Manuel has learned a lesson from the judge is

A "nods his head vigorously in assent"

B "goes into bakery"

C "opens his cash box"

D "curtain closes"

4 Imagine that Manuel is describing the lesson he learned at the end of the play to someone. Tell this lesson in several sentences.

_____

_____

_____

_____

5 Do you think that the best things in life are free? Explain your answer.

_____

_____

_____

_____

Reading Objective: Apply a variety of reading strategies.
Writing Objective: Continue to respond actively and imaginatively to literature.

Tennessee

Name _____

Steps in a Process

Writing that tells how to reach a goal or make something may give the steps in a process. When you are asked to identify these steps on a test, look for clue words such as *first, next,* and *last* which show order, and try to picture the step as you read.

Here is a simple art project to do inside on a rainy day. First, collect materials. You will need a large piece of cardboard or thick paper; pictures from magazines; paper of different colors; small objects such as buttons, macaroni, or pebbles; and glue; scissors. Cut the paper and pictures into different shapes and sizes. Next, take a large piece of cardboard or thick paper and draw a frame around the outside. Glue the cut paper and pictures onto the cardboard to make a figure or an original design. Finally, decorate your artwork with small objects, using them as eyes, borders, flowers, or background. Let the project dry for about 12 hours. Don't forget to sign your masterpiece!

1 The first thing you should do to start this project is

A collect materials

B find a piece of cardboard

C cut the paper and pictures

D glue the paper and pictures to the board

2 Which of the following steps do you do before drawing a frame on the board?

F cut the paper and pictures

G glue the paper and pictures

H let the project dry

J sign the artwork

3 Which of the following steps does <u>not</u> come before you decorate your artwork?

A go outside

B draw a frame on the board

C let the glue dry

D press the board flat

4 Describe one additional step you could add to the art project.

_____

_____

_____

_____

_____

© Scott Foresman 5

Tennessee

Reading Objective: Apply a variety of reading strategies.
Writing Objective: Continue to respond actively and imaginatively to literature.

Name _____

Steps in a Process

Read "Andy's Secret Ingredient" (pages 583–594). Then answer the questions below.

1 What is the first thing Andy does to prepare for his essay?

A He goes to a diner with his Dad.

B He eats grubs and worms.

C He writes to an insect professor.

D He asks his Mom what *bon appetit* means.

2 Page 592 describes how Andy collects and cares for beetles. What does he do right after he collects them in a jar?

F He puts them in a screened cage.

G He fills half a jar.

H He carries the jar up to his room.

J He puts cornmeal in the cage.

3 Before Andy chops the beetles, he does everything except

A puts them in a cookie tin

B freezes them

C feeds them cornmeal

D toasts them in the oven

4 What does Andy add to the batter immediately before he adds the beetles?

F flour

G eggs

H sugar

J walnuts

5 Read "Bug-a-licious!" (pages 597–599). Imagine that Andy attended the Bug Bowl. How would he fit in with the scientists? Explain what his experience might be like.

_____

_____

_____

_____

_____

_____

_____

_____

_____

Reading Objective: Apply a variety of reading strategies.
Writing Objective: Continue to respond actively and imaginatively to literature.

Tennessee

Name _____

Steps in a Process

Read "Andy's Secret Ingredient" (pages 583–594). Then answer the questions below.

1 Before he can start his project, Andy

 A pulls their wings and legs off and chops them

 B shares his brownies with his classmates

 C asks his aunt whether she would eat a bug

 D writes to an insect professor for advice

2 Immediately after Andy puts his beetles in a cage, he

 F hides the jar and takes it to his room

 G freezes them

 H mixes them with walnuts

 J feeds them cornmeal

3 Which choice best describes the steps Wendell takes to eat the brownie?

 A swallows a bite, looks at it, eats the rest

 B looks at it, swallows three bites in a row

 C takes one bite, looks at it, and throws the rest away

 D chews a bite, swallows it, eats the rest of the brownie without looking at it

4 Write a recipe card that shows the steps you need to make beetle brownies.

_____

_____

_____

_____

5 Read "Bug-a-licious!" (pages 597–599). Explain what steps Andy could have taken to make another treat.

_____

_____

_____

_____

_____

Reading Objective: Apply a variety of reading strategies.
Writing Objective: Continue to respond actively and imaginatively to literature.

Tennessee

Name _____

Plot

Test questions may ask about a story's plot, or important events. Look for the conflict, or main problem, in the story and think about how it is resolved. Think also about the climax, or high point, of the story.

Hattie invited her family for Thanksgiving. The highlight of the meal was to be a juicy, brown turkey. She prepared the turkey by seasoning it and stuffing it with dressing. Then she roasted it for 6 hours in the oven. Just before she served the turkey, Hattie put it on a platter. When the moment arrived to feed her guests, she carried the turkey from the kitchen. But she stepped on some butter that had dropped on the floor. She slipped and the turkey slid from the platter onto the floor. The guests were speechless, but Hattie knew just what to say. "Don't worry. I'll be back in a minute with the other turkey." Everyone laughed and enjoyed the meal.

1 **What is the climax of the story?**

A Hattie invites her family for Thanksgiving.

B Hattie makes a joke.

C Hattie drops the turkey on the floor.

D Hattie roasts the turkey for hours.

2 **What detail does not affect the plot?**

F Hattie steps in butter.

G Hattie slips.

H The turkey slides from the platter.

J Hattie stuffs the turkey.

3 **Hattie resolves her problem by**

A dropping the turkey

B making another turkey

C joking about it

D slipping on the floor

4 **Do you think that Hattie resolved the conflict of the story well, or could you suggest a better solution? Explain.**

_____

_____

_____

_____

_____

_____

_____

_____

Tennessee

Reading Objective: Apply a variety of reading strategies.
Writing Objective: Continue to respond actively and imaginatively to literature.

Name _____

● Plot

Read "In the Days of King Adobe" (pages 603–611). Then answer the questions below.

1 What problem is the old woman trying to solve in this story?

A She wants to make dinner for her guests.

B She wants more money so she can buy more food.

C She wants to trick the young men into giving her money.

D She wants to stop the young men from stealing her ham.

2 Which of the following is <u>not</u> important to the plot?

F The old woman watches what the young men are doing.

G The old woman sells vegetables in the village.

H The old woman puts a brick in their traveling bag.

J The old woman tells them about her dream.

3 Which choice best describes the climax of this story?

A The young men discover that they have been tricked.

B The young men eat breakfast with the old woman.

C The young men are hungry.

D The young men tell the story of Adobe the Great.

4 The outcome of the story is

F the young men continue to trick old women who feed them well

G the young men learn not to trick people who help them

H the old woman takes revenge on the young men by stealing their ham

J the old woman continues to tell excellent stories and cook good food

5 Describe a possible outcome of the story if the old woman had <u>not</u> discovered the young men's trick. What will happen to the young men and the old woman?

_____

_____

_____

_____

_____

_____

_____

Name _____

Plot

Read "In the Days of King Adobe" (pages 603–611). Then answer the questions below.

1 Which of the following is <u>not</u> important to the outcome in this story?

A The old woman watches the young men steal her ham.

B The old woman replaces the ham with an adobe brick.

C The old woman tells the young men about her dream.

D The young men awake in the morning.

2 The problem the old woman in this story is trying to solve is

F she doesn't have enough food to feed the young men

G the young men want to steal her ham

H she wants to trick the young men so that she can laugh

J the young men won't listen to her dream

3 Which choice best describes the outcome of this story?

A The young men do not steal.

B The young men return the ham.

C The young men are hungry.

D The young men steal the ham.

4 Describe the climax of the story in your own words.

_____

_____

_____

5 Think about a story, fable, or myth in which tricking someone is part of the plot. Give a brief summary of the plot.

_____

_____

_____

© Scott Foresman 5

Reading Objective: Improve comprehension by interpreting, analyzing, synthesizing, and evaluating written text.
Writing Objective: Write frequently for a variety of purposes such as narration, and description.

Tennessee

Name

Making Judgments

Making judgments means forming opinions about something or someone. When a test asks you to make judgments about a character or idea, look for evidence in the text.

Mei's mother called her a "fussy eater" because she rarely ate everything on her plate. When Mrs. Teng asked Mei if the food was too spicy or too plain, Mei shrugged her shoulders and said, "I'm just not very hungry, I guess. We have the same things every week." One day Mei was invited to dinner at her friend Lili's house. When she came home, she said, "Mom, I had three helpings tonight. Lili and I got to make dinner, and it was delicious." She explained that the girls had made little pizzas. They cut bagels into three slices and put tomato sauce and cheese on each slice. Then family members added their favorite things on top—pepperoni, vegetables, and olives. Mei said, "Then we had a great fruit salad. Lili and I put grapes and pieces of melon on toothpicks. It looked so pretty and tasted good. Why can't we have pizza and fruit at our house, Mom?" Mrs. Teng said, "Mei, we do have pizza and fruit at our house. But you have never prepared it yourself in a special way. Tomorrow, you can help me make a grocery list. I'll shop and buy the food you want. You can help prepare it and add your special touches. After all, preparing a meal yourself can make the food taste better."

1 The word that best describes Mei in the beginning of the story is

A fussy

B bored

C hungry

D angry

2 Mei likes the dinner at Lili's because

F she hasn't eaten all day

G it's the first time she eats pizza

H Lili's family lets her eat what she wants

J she helps prepare it, and it seems different

3 Which answer best completes the chart?

Questions	Judgment	Support
What does Mei's mother decide?	?	Mei doesn't enjoy meals prepared only by her mother. Mei enjoyed the meal she fixed at Lili's.

A Mei enjoys meals if she helps plan and make them.

B Mei's mother will fix pizza every night.

C Mei will do all the shopping.

D Mei will only eat fruit salad.

4 Do you think Mei's mother has made a reasonable judgment about Mei? Explain.

_____

_____

_____

Reading Objective: Improve comprehension by interpreting, analyzing, synthesizing, and evaluating written text.
Writing Objective: Write frequently for a variety of purposes such as narration, and description.

Tennessee

Name _____

Making Judgments

Read "Just Telling the Truth" (pages 617–633). Then answer the questions below.

1 Which word best describes Felicia's character?

A smart

B critical

C mean

D helpful

2 Felicia has problems dealing with her friends at school because she

F is mean to them on purpose

G never comes to school

H ignores them all the time

J does not realize that she upsets them

3 According to pages 629–630, Felicia shows that she understands the value of constructive criticism by

A not telling people what she thinks

B writing her criticisms in a notebook

C forcing Marilyn to see the new closet

D reorganizing the broom closet

4 Which choice supports the conclusion that Felicia's mother likes the new closet?

F "Marilyn complained, but she came, finally, into the kitchen too."

G "Felicia beamed with pride."

H "Felicia, it's wonderful."

J "Hold the unveiling without me."

5 How do you think the author feels about Felicia? Use examples from the text to support your judgments.

_____

_____

_____

_____

_____

_____

_____

_____

Tennessee

Reading Objective: Improve comprehension by interpreting, analyzing, synthesizing, and evaluating written text.
Writing Objective: Write frequently for a variety of purposes such as narration, and description.

Name _____

Making Judgments

Read "Just Telling the Truth" (pages 617–633). Then answer the questions below.

1 Which detail does <u>not</u> indicate that Felicia is critical?

A She tells Cheryl she's late.

B She trades sandwiches with Cheryl.

C She suggests that Cheryl put a sign next to her alarm clock.

D She says how the crossing guard should direct traffic.

2 Phyllis, Lorraine, and Fern are angry with Felicia because she

F is mean to them on purpose.

G joins Wendy Frank's club

H ignores them at lunch

J does not give constructive criticism

3 According to Felicia's mother, what is *constructive criticism*?

A telling other people what their faults are

B fixing closets

C explaining why your opinion is the best one

D making positive suggestions about how things can be done better

4 What do you think of Felicia's sister? Describe Marilyn's character and use examples from the text to support your judgment.

_____

_____

_____

_____

5 Would you like to have Felicia for a friend? Use examples from the text to support your judgments.

_____

_____

_____

_____

© Scott Foresman 5

Reading Objective: Apply a variety of reading strategies.
Writing Objective: Continue to respond actively and imaginatively to literature.

Tennessee

Name _____

Visualizing

Visualizing is making a picture in your mind as you read. On a test you may be asked to identify ways an author helps you visualize things in a story. In answering, think about descriptions of how things look, smell, sound, taste, or feel.

My favorite painting is in the first room of the Art Museum. Its title is *Girl in a Garden*. A French artist painted it over 100 years ago. There is a smiling girl about six years old sitting on a large white chair in a garden full of red roses and white poppies. She is wearing a straw hat with daisies on the brim. You can tell it is a windy day because the streamers on her hat and her hair look like they are blowing. A fluffy white dog is sleeping on her lap. To her left is a cherry tree full of pink blossoms. In front of the girl is a bowl of red apples.

1 **All of the colors below are mentioned in this article except**

  A red

  B white

  C pink

  D gray

2 **In this passage the girl probably feels**

  F happy

  G angry

  H curious

  J hungry

3 **Which answer best completes the empty box?**

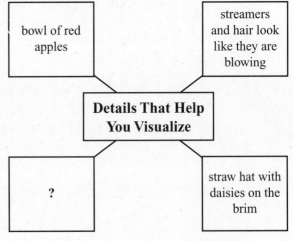

  A painted over 100 years ago

  B fluffy white dog sleeping on her lap

  C Art Museum

  D favorite painting

4 **Would you like to have *Girl in a Garden* hanging in your room? Explain why or why not.**

_____

_____

_____

_____

Tennessee

Reading Objective: Apply a variety of reading strategies.
Writing Objective: Continue to respond actively and imaginatively to literature.

Name _____

● Visualizing

Read "Is It Real?" (pages 639–647). Then answer the questions below.

1 Marilyn Levine's *Black Gloves* is

  A a book that teaches the reader about the *trompe l'oeil* movement

  B a ceramic artwork that looks like leather gloves

  C the artist's work gloves that she wears while creating her sculptures

  D an artistic movement from the 1980s and 1990s

2 Which choice best describes the piece called *Traveler*?

  F photos from a recent trip to Europe

  G a man sitting in an airplane

  H a sleeping traveler with bags

  J a porter carrying a suitcase

3 *Strawberry Tart Supreme* appeals mostly to which of the following senses?

  A sight and sound

  B smell and sound

  C taste and sound

  D sight and taste

4 Which choice best describes what *trompe l'oeil* is?

  F sculpture that shows everyday items such as gloves

  G art that dates back to the ancient Greeks

  H trash under a rug

  J art meant to trick the viewers' eyes

5 **Read "See the Picture!" (pages 650–653). Describe what happens in your eye when you look at Audrey Flack's *Strawberry Tart Supreme* (page 645).**

_____

_____

_____

_____

_____

_____

_____

_____

_____

_____

Tennessee
Reading Objective: Apply a variety of reading strategies.
Writing Objective: Continue to respond actively and imaginatively to literature.

Name _____

Visualizing

Read "Is It Real?" (pages 639–647). Then answer the questions below.

1 What choice best describes Duane Hanson's *Traveler*?

A a book that teaches the reader about *trompe l'oeil*

B a life-size sculpture that looks like a real person sleeping

C a photograph of an exhausted man sitting in an airport

D an artistic movement from the 1980s and 1990s

2 Which words do <u>not</u> help you visualize *Strawberry Tart Supreme*?

F gooey, sweet desserts

G chocolate icing

H whipped cream and strawberries

J interesting food

3 Which choice would be the best example of *trompe l'oeil* art?

A a very small painting of a frog that must be seen with a microscope

B a photograph of a large, green frog

C a watercolor of a frog with many drips and water marks

D a green ceramic frog made to look real

4 Read the description of *Pups in Transit* on page 644. Name at least two words or phrases that help you visualize the painting. Explain how those phrases help you imagine the artwork.

_____

_____

_____

_____

5 Look at Kent Addison's *Still Life* (page 647). Describe this artwork so that someone else can visualize it.

_____

_____

_____

_____

Test-Taking Strategies and Skills

Notes to the Teacher

The Test-Taking Strategies and Skills pages provide practice using the TCAP test format and will help you prepare students for the TCAP test administered in fifth grade. Use the Test-Taking Strategies and Skills pages in several sittings before you administer the TCAP practice test. You can photocopy the Test-Taking Strategies and Skills blackline masters in advance and prepare a booklet for each student. Attach a blank sheet of paper to the front of each booklet for a cover. Have students write their names on their covers. You may wish do one or two questions as a whole class to make sure students understand how to use the suggested strategy. Additional strategies and test-taking tips are given below.

Additional Strategies

Pacing   Teach students these time-management formulas for test taking.

Multiple-Choice Tests   Divide the total number of test questions by the total number of minutes allowed for the test. This will tell you how much time to allow for each question.

Writing Tests   Allow about 10 percent of the time to decide on a topic. Allow about 80 percent of the time to prewrite and write. (Generally, some students need more time to prewrite, while others need more time to write. Therefore, students should decide individually how to divide this 80 percent block of time.) Allow about 10 percent of the time to proofread.

Guess or Skip   When students are unsure of an answer to a question on a standardized test, they can either guess the answer or skip the question. It is best to guess answers on tests for which scores are based on the total number of correct answers compared to the total number of questions (whether answered or not). It is best to skip the questions on tests for which scores are based on the total number of correct answers compared to the total number of questions answered. Determine in advance which type of test you're administering and tell your students whether to guess or skip.

Rethinking Answers   Students can rethink their answers on a multiple-choice test if they finish early. However, if they have already carefully thought through all the answer choices, then their first answer is more likely to be correct than a changed answer.

Test-Taking Tips

Remind your students of these tips:
1. Be well rested and eat a nutritious breakfast.
2. Remember to write your name on the test.
3. Always read the test directions. Ask your teacher if you don't understand something.
4. Relax! Do your best and enjoy the challenge.

Answer Key

Test-Taking Strategies and Skills

Preread the Title and Questions
1. A
2. J
3. B
4. H
5. A
6. H

Read, Think, Look
1. D
2. H
3. C
4. G
5. A
6. H

X-It, Circle, and Return
1. B
2. F
3. A
4. H
5. B
6. F

Answering Literal Questions
1. C
2. G
3. D
4. G
5. A
6. G

Reading Long Passages: Break It Down
1. B
2. F

Reading Long Passages: Ask Yourself Questions
1. Possible answers: Pamela likes horses. Pamela's favorite activity is going to riding lessons and practicing jumping. Pamela received a horse named Misty for her eleventh birthday.
2. Possible answer: Pamela was concerned about her summer vacation because she isn't sure how much riding she will be able to do.
3. Questions and answers will vary, but should relate to information in the last part of the passage. Possible question: What will probably happen next? Possible answer: Pamela spends a happy summer with Misty, at Oak Hill Horse Camp, practicing jumping.

Answering Word-Meaning Questions
1. D
2. H
3. A
4. H
5. D
6. G

Answering Fill-in-the-Blank Questions
1. A
2. J
3. B
4. G
5. B

Answering "Not" and "Except" Questions
1. C
2. F
3. A
4. J
5. B

Answering Language Questions
1. A
2. G
3. D
4. G
5. D
6. H

Examine and Decide
Top Chart What to Write: about a dream that came true, a detailed story; Audience: kids in my school
Bottom Chart Answers will vary.

Prewrite
Charts will vary.

Write a Sample
Samples need to correspond to the prewriting charts.

Proofread
1. D
2. B
Proofreading will vary according to each writing sample.

Preparing for Standardized Tests
Preread the Title and Questions

Before you answer questions about a passage on a standardized test, it is helpful to *preread the title and questions*. This will give you clues about the passage. The clues will help you read the passage faster and understand it better.

The following are the title and most of the questions that go with the reading passage on the next page. For each item, fill in the circle next to the clue that the title or question gives you.

1 **Title: The Big Ride**

- **A** The title tells me that the passage is about some kind of big ride.
- **B** The title tells me that the passage is about people who take a car ride.
- **C** The title tells me that the passage is about people who take a boat ride.
- **D** The title doesn't give any clues.

2 **Where does this story probably take place?**

- **F** This question tells me where the story takes place.
- **G** This question tells me that it rains in the story.
- **H** This question tells me that the passage is about a group of fifth-graders.
- **J** This question doesn't give any clues.

3 **Why was Freddy so scared?**

- **A** This question tells me that Freddy laughs in the story.
- **B** This question tells me that Freddy was scared about something.
- **C** This question tells me that Freddy is very brave.
- **D** This question doesn't give any clues.

4 **Why did Freddy agree to go on the roller coaster?**

- **F** This question tells me that Freddy is a coward.
- **G** This question tells me that Freddy loves fast cars.
- **H** This question tells me that Freddy agrees to go on a roller coaster.
- **J** This question doesn't give any clues.

5 **What did Freddy's friends tell him to do?**

- **A** This question tells me that Freddy's friends tell him to do something.
- **B** This question tells me that Freddy's friends are friendly.
- **C** This question tells me that Freddy has no friends.
- **D** This question doesn't give any clues.

6 **What does the word *secured* mean?**

- **F** I have no idea. I'm going to fail.
- **G** I'll ask my teacher what secured means.
- **H** I need to find the word secured in the passage and underline it if it isn't already darkened.
- **J** I need to guess now what the word secured means.

Read, Think, Look

After you have preread the title and questions for a reading passage, read the passage. Then follow these steps to answer the questions: **(1)** *Read* the question. **(2)** Cover up the answers with a piece of paper and *think* of the answer in your head. **(3)** *Look* at the answers and choose the one that comes closest to your own. If you're not sure of an answer, you can always look back at the passage.

You have already preread the title and most of the questions on the page before. Now read the passage. Then read, think, look, and choose your answer.

The Big Ride

I didn't want my friends to think I was strange, so I went along with it, even though I was secretly terrified. "Relax, Freddy!" they told me. But I was thinking more about just surviving. When the operator secured the safety bar over my lap, I knew that there was no turning back. Soon the roller coaster ride began, and I squeezed my eyes shut. It was over in a flash. I was amazed at how much fun it was. I'll keep my eyes open next time.

1 Where does this story probably take place?

A at a shopping mall

B at the gas station

C on a mountain

D at an amusement park

2 What was Freddy afraid of?

F He was afraid of heights.

G His friends made him afraid.

H He was afraid of the roller coaster ride.

J He was afraid he would get lost.

3 Why did Freddy agree to go on the roller coaster?

A He loved roller coasters.

B He wanted to get his money's worth.

C He didn't want to seem odd to his friends.

D His friends dared him to go on it.

4 What did Freddy's friends tell him to do?

F to keep his eyes shut

G to relax

H to scream

J to stay home

5 What does the word *secured* mean?

A put firmly in place

B unlocked

C put loosely in place

D removed

6 What will Freddy probably do next time he goes to the amusement park?

F stay off of the roller coaster

G warn others about the roller coaster

H enjoy the roller coaster

J keep his eyes closed on the roller coaster

X-It, Circle, and Return

If you are unsure of an answer, do the following: **(1)** Write a light *X* after each answer choice that you know is not correct. **(2)** *Circle* the question number. **(3)** *Return* to it when you have finished the page and choose an answer that does not have an *X* after it. See the example below.

1 **Choose the sentence that has the article underlined.**

A The crystal vase is cracked.

B The crystal vase is cracked. X

C The crystal vase is cracked. X

D The crystal vase is cracked.

First, skim the questions. Then read, think, look, and choose your answer. For answers that you are unsure of, *X*-it, circle, and return.

1 **Which of the following is spelled correctly?**

A interferince

B interference

C interrference

D interferense

2 **What is the meaning of the word *maxilla?***

F a jaw or jawbone

G very big

H a kind of gorilla

J the cells of a beehive

3 **What is a paraphrase?**

A a restatement in other words

B part of a phrase from a book

C a song lyric

D two phrases in the same paragraph

4 **What is an inference?**

F the static on your radio

G an interference

H an opinion or judgment based on facts

J a question

5 **Which of the following is spelled correctly?**

A litterature

B literature

C literrture

D literture

6 **Choose the sentence that has the preposition underlined.**

F I put my book on the table, and it stayed there.

G I put my book on the table, and it stayed there.

H I put my book on the table, and it stayed there.

J I put my book on the table, and it stayed there.

Return to each of the numbers you circled. Choose an answer that does not have an *X* after it. Guess only if you need to.

© Scott Foresman 5

Answering Literal Questions
Skim to Find

A literal question asks about something that is stated exactly in a passage that you've read. When you're unsure of the answer, *skim* the passage *to find* the answer. To skim, look for a certain word or number without reading every word.

Read the passage. For each question, skim to find and choose the correct answer.

These are the directions we follow to get to my cousin Chris's house. First, we turn right onto Willow Path Road, and we drive for about two-and-a-half miles. Then, we turn left onto Mango Street, and we drive for about four miles. After four miles, we turn left onto Klipter Road. We drive west on Klipter Road for about one-and-a-quarter miles, and then we veer north onto Roosevelt Avenue. We drive for about ten minutes on Roosevelt, and when we come to the Prangler Shopping Center, we turn right at the next light. This puts us on Hippity Road going east. Chris lives on Hippity Road very close to the shopping center.

1 What street do we turn right onto first?

A Mango Street

B Klipter Road

C Willow Path Road

D Roosevelt Avenue

2 On what street do we drive one-and-a-quarter miles?

F Mango Street

G Klipter Road

H Roosevelt Avenue

J Hippity Road

3 Onto what street do we veer north?

A Mango Street

B Prangler Shopping Center

C Klipter Road

D Roosevelt Avenue

4 For how long do we drive on Roosevelt Avenue?

F about five minutes

G about ten minutes

H about fifteen minutes

J about twenty minutes

5 What direction do we turn at the light after the Prangler Shopping Center?

A right

B left

C west

D We don't turn here.

6 On what street is Chris's house?

F Prangler Center

G Hippity Road

H Roosevelt Avenue

J Willow Path Road

© Scott Foresman 5

Reading Long Passages
Break It Down

When you read a long passage, break it down into smaller parts. Stop after each paragraph to make sure you understand what it is about. You can do this by underlining the main idea or writing key words in the margin. If you have trouble understanding a paragraph, read it again more slowly.

Read the passage. As you read, underline the important ideas in each paragraph and write key words in the margin that summarize what you have learned.

Guide Dogs

Guide dogs are strong and intelligent working dogs. They have an important job to do. They help people who are visually impaired (people who have trouble seeing) travel safely. Guide dogs help their human partners walk around their neighborhoods, cross the streets, and even ride subways and buses.

Training guide dogs to do this job takes a lot of time and work. Learning the special skills needed to be a guide dog takes four months of training. Each day the dogs learn new skills. They learn to stop at curbs and stairs and to avoid objects in their way.

Guide dogs react to commands given to them. The humans tell them which way to go and when to cross the street. One of the most important skills the dogs learn is to disobey dangerous commands given to them. For example, the visually impaired person may not know that a car has run a red light and may give the dog a signal to cross. The guide dog's job is to help hold the person at the curb until it is safe.

Key Words

1 **When should guide dogs disobey their human friends?**

A when they want to eat

B when a command may lead to danger

C when they want to cross the street on their own

D when they are on the subway

2 **The purpose of this passage is to**

F describe what a guide dog does

G tell what guide dogs look like

H show that people need help too

J explain that dogs are as smart as people

© Scott Foresman 5

Reading Long Passages
Ask Yourself Questions

A good way to read long passages is to pause as you read and ask yourself questions that will help you better understand what you are reading. Ask yourself questions such as: "What have I learned?," "What do I think will happen next?," "What does this event tell me about this character?," and "Why did this happen?"

Answer the questions about the first two parts. For the last part, write your own question about it. Then write an answer.

Pamela's Summer Plan

Pamela flipped through her favorite magazine, *Horse and Rider*. She thought about her upcoming summer vacation. She was wondering how often she would be able to ride her horse, Misty. She had received Misty a year ago as a present for her eleventh birthday.

Pamela's favorite activity was going to riding lessons and practicing jumping. She thought that she'd like to compete in jumping events someday. She imagined herself competing in front of a big crowd. She thought it would be an exciting challenge.

1 **Question: What are three things I have learned about Pamela?**

Answer: _____

_____

Pamela was worried about how much riding she could do over the summer, though. Her riding teacher, Ms. Hughes, was on vacation for most of the summer. Pamela wasn't ready to take out her horse by herself yet so she needed a plan. Pamela loved Ms. Hughes. No one could really replace her, but she still hoped she could find someone to teach her just for the summer.

2 **Question: Why was Pamela concerned about her summer vacation?**

Answer: _____

_____

Suddenly an ad in the magazine caught her eye. As she read it, she realized how she and Misty could spend the entire summer together. She ran into the living room to show her parents the ad for Oak Hill Horse Camp. It was just a few miles from their home. She was sure her parents would think this camp was a great idea too.

3 Question: _____

_____

Answer: _____

_____

© Scott Foresman 5

Answering Word-Meaning Questions
Use Context Clues

When you are asked to find the meaning of a word in a passage, *use context clues*. To do this, first skim the passage to find the word. Then read what is written before and after the word to figure out its meaning.

First, read the passage. Then, use context clues to figure out the meanings of the nonsense words. Finally, choose the correct answer.

What a day to remember! We arrived at school at four o'clock in the morning and were off on our trip to the state capital forty-five minutes later. After riding on the tour fratyon for two-and-a-half hours, we ate a quick breakfast at a nortom food place. It was only seven-fifteen in the morning, and we were all anticipating a phenomenal day. Three hours later we wimmed at our destination. Would you believe that we saw the hetby in the capitol building? Well, after a dod day of touring and another long bus ride home, we returned exhausted. It was a runder none of us will ever forget.

1 **What is another word for** *fratyon?*

- **A** schedule
- **B** truck
- **C** group
- **D** bus

2 **What is another word for** *nortom?*

- **F** gourmet
- **G** fancy
- **H** fast
- **J** closed

3 **What is another word for** *wimmed?*

- **A** arrived
- **B** called
- **C** departed
- **D** left

4 **What is another word for** *hetby?*

- **F** songwriter
- **G** grocer
- **H** governor
- **J** artist

5 **What is another word for** *dod?*

- **A** boring
- **B** glad
- **C** sad
- **D** thrilling

6 **What is another word for** *runder?*

- **F** song
- **G** trip
- **H** number
- **J** name

Answering Fill-in-the-Blank Questions
Try and Choose

To answer a fill-in-the-blank question on a standardized test, first read the test item with the blank that needs to be filled. Then *try* to fit every answer choice into the blank. Write a light *X* after answers that don't fit. *Choose* the answer that does fit.

For each fill-in-the-blank question, try every answer choice. Then choose the correct one.

1 **Read the story and decide which sentence fills in the blank best.**

> Alicia's parents said she could take an art class after school. First, she found out about classes offered in her neighborhood. Then, she called to register. _____. She brought everything she needed to the second class.

A At the first class they told her what supplies to purchase.

B Later, she decided not to take the class.

C Finally, she finished her first project.

D Next, she found out about art classes.

2 **Choose the best topic sentence.**

> _____. He was convinced he would conquer his opponents. After all, he'd been studying and practicing for over two months. Phil's only concern was the possibility of being asked to spell an obsolete word that he had never heard of before. Nevertheless, he felt equipped to spell just about any word.

F The day of the science fair finally arrived.

G Many fifth graders entered the music competition.

H Phil was prepared for the geography contest.

J Phil was prepared for the spelling bee.

3 **Choose the word that fits in <u>both</u> blanks.**

> *I hope the _____ didn't _____ the poison.*

A inspector

B swallow

C container

D liquid

4 **Which word completes the sentence best?**

> *The treasure was _____ on the summit.*

F hided

G hidden

H hide

J hider

5 **Choose the word that fits in <u>both</u> blanks.**

> *The _____ had apple _____ for dessert.*

A pie

B cobbler

C juice

D banker

Answering "Not" and "Except" Questions

Cover Up and Restate

When you are given a question with *not* or *except,* cover up the word *not* or the phrase with *except.* Then restate the question. You can restate Question 2 as "Which of the following does describe where Max lives?" Write an *X* lightly after the three choices that answer the restated question. The remaining choice will be the answer for the "not" question.

Read the passage. For each question, cover up the word *not* or the phrase *except which one.* Restate the question. Write an *X* after the three choices that answer the restated question. Then choose the answer without an *X* after it.

It was a difficult day for Max. He was feeling really down. Today Max was moving from Nashville to a small town outside the city. He was leaving all of his friends, and had to get used to a new school and a new kind of place to live. Max liked the city noise and seeing lots of people on the streets. He loved going to the park across the street from his apartment. His mom told him it might be hard at first, but that he would get used to living in a smaller town soon, make new friends, and have fun playing in his own backyard. He hoped his mother was right.

1 Which of the following does <u>not</u> describe how Max is feeling?

A gloomy

B sad

C excited

D depressed

2 Which of the following does <u>not</u> describe where Max lives now?

F He lives in a house with a yard.

G He lives across the street from a park.

H He lives in an apartment.

J He lives in Nashville.

3 Which of the following does <u>not</u> describe where Max is moving to?

A a city

B a small town

C outside of Nashville

D a house with a yard

4 All of the following are reasons Max was upset except which one?

F He was leaving all of his friends.

G He was going to miss the park.

H He had to go to a new school.

J He was going to have a new backyard.

5 Max's mother encourages him with all of the following reasons except which one?

A He will make new friends.

B He will have a better room.

C He will have fun in his new backyard.

D He will get used to his new town soon.

Answering Language Questions
Think It Through

To answer language questions, *think through* every answer choice. Then choose the correct answer. See the example in the chart below.

Question	Think It Through
Which sentence has the contraction underlined?	I'll think through every answer choice.
A My <u>friend's</u> dog isn't much fun.	The word *friend's* is a possessive.
B My friend's <u>dog</u> isn't much fun.	The word *dog* is not a contraction.
C My friend's dog <u>isn't</u> much fun.	The word *isn't* is a contraction, but I'll read the last answer choice just in case.
D My friend's dog isn't <u>much</u> fun.	The word *much* is not a contraction. *C* has to be the correct answer.

For each question, think through every answer choice. Then choose the correct answer.

1 **Which sentence has the proper noun underlined?**

    A <u>Marta</u> scored ten points for her team.

    B Marta scored ten points <u>for</u> her team.

    C Marta scored ten points for <u>her</u> team.

    D Marta scored ten points for her <u>team</u>.

2 **Which sentence has the apostrophe in the correct place?**

    F The cheerleaders' shoelace untied at a crucial moment.

    G The cheerleaders' coach invited them to a picnic.

    H The coachs' attitude encouraged the team.

    J The waiters' pen fell next to his foot on the linoleum floor.

3 **What word is missing?**

    My cousin _____ me to go on the rafting trip.

    A persuading

    B is persuaded

    C did persuaded

    D persuaded

4 **Which sentence is correct?**

    F The clock isn't running no more.

    G My brother and I never go fishing anymore.

    H You won't get nowhere without a map.

    J I never did run no mile.

5 **Which sentence is correct?**

    A Washington, State is very mountainous.

    B My uncle graduated from Colorado, State, University.

    C West, Virginia is a southeastern state.

    D It took us eight hours to drive to Ann Arbor, Michigan.

6 **Which sentence has the pronoun underlined?**

    F <u>The</u> queen admired her own majestic crown.

    G The <u>queen</u> admired her own majestic crown.

    H The queen admired <u>her</u> own majestic crown.

    J The queen admired her <u>own</u> majestic crown.

© Scott Foresman 5

Preparing for Writing Tests
Step 1: Examine and Decide

Examine the Prompt Before you begin a writing test, examine the prompt to figure out what it is asking you to write and who your audience is.

See the example below and complete the chart.

Writing Prompt	What to Write	Audience
A. Think back to a time you would like to relive. Write a story for your teacher telling what happened. Use details.	1. about a time I would like to relive 2. tell what happened 3. use details	my teacher
B. Everyone has dreams he or she wish would come true. Imagine that one of your dreams did come true. For your school newspaper, write a detailed story about your dream that came true.	_____ _____ _____	_____ _____ _____

Decide on a Topic After you have examined the writing prompt, you need to decide on a topic. One way to do this is to write a list of topic ideas. Then review your list and decide which one to write about. The chart below gives an example of how to do this for writing prompt *A* in the above chart.

List of Possible Topics	Decide
1. our family trip to Alaska	There's too much to say about this.
2. when I won the spelling bee	This was great! I could say a lot.
3. when I taught myself how to whistle	This isn't a very interesting topic. I'll write about the spelling bee.

Fill in the chart for writing promt *B*. First, write a list of possible topics. Then, write to show how you decide.

List of Possible Topics	Decide
_____ _____ _____	_____ _____ _____

Step 2: Prewrite

When you have decided on a topic, the next step is to prewrite. There are various ways to prewrite. They include: writing an outline, making a web, drawing a picture, and making a chart.

To make a chart, follow these steps: **(1)** Decide what ideas you'll use to tell about your topic. Place these ideas in the column headings. **(2)** Decide what details you'll use to support each idea. Place these in the rows underneath the column headings. **(3)** Number your heading ideas and details in the right sequence or in order from least important to most important.

See the example below for the spelling bee topic on page 103.

Prepared for 3 Months (1)	The Contest (2)	Afterwards (3)
used the dictionary (2)	very nervous at first (1)	was in the newspaper (2)
Dan was my coach (1)	kept answering right (2)	got a trophy (1)
practiced every day (3)	won with *distraught* (3)	went to the state capital (3)

Make a prewriting chart below for the topic you chose on page 103.

© Scott Foresman 5

Step 3: Write a Sample

When you are ready to write a sample, use your prewriting to organize your paper and to see what details to include. As you write, remember to do the following: **(1)** Write a topic sentence and conclusion sentence that are both interesting. **(2)** Make sure that each sentence relates to your topic. **(3)** Skip lines to leave room for proofreading.

Read the writing sample below and compare it to the prewriting chart on page 104.

It would be exciting to relive the time I won our school spelling bee. I prepared for the contest for three months. My best friend Dan was my coach. Dan and I used the dictionary to find challenging words for me to learn. We practiced every day.

When the spelling bee started, I was quite nervous. I became more relaxed as I continued to spell the words I was given correctly. I won with the word *distraught*, which means "upset."

After I won I was awarded a huge bronze trophy. Then reporters took my photograph for the newspaper. The best part was that I got to go to our state capital to compete in the state spelling bee. I would love to relive the whole thing if I could.

Use your own prewriting chart on page 104 to write a sample on the lines below. If you run out of room, use the back of the page.

_____

_____

_____

_____

_____

_____

_____

_____

_____

_____

_____

Step 4: Proofread

PROOFREADING TIPS	
What to Check	**What to Do**
topic sentence conclusion sentence	Make sure the first sentence is indented and introduces your topic. Make sure the last sentence is a good ending.
sentences that don't relate to topic	Take these out.
missing words, grammar, punctuation, capitalization, indenting	Read each sentence, starting with the last one first. Look for errors and correct them. Make sure the first sentence of each paragraph is indented.
spelling	Correct all spelling errors.

First, read the writing sample below. Then, answer the proofreading questions. Finally, proofread your own writing sample on page 105, and use the above chart to make corrections.

One of the best times of my life was when my friend Sharia and I prepared for the double-dutch jump rope contest and won. We practiced every day after school. The new moves and tricks we created were impressive. My sister Patrice enjoys running races instead.

The day of the contest finally arrived, and the contest soon began. At first I was nervous, but then the cheering crowd put me at ease. We won after an intense hour of competition. After the contest Sharia and I became celebrities in our school. Everyone wanted to be our friend. That entire experience was one of the best times in my life.

1 **What should be indented to begin a new paragraph?**

A We practiced every day

B The new moves and tricks

C We won

D After the contest

2 **Which sentence does _not_ belong?**

F We practiced every day after school.

G My sister Patrice enjoys running races instead.

H We won after an intense hour of competition.

J Everyone wanted to be our friend.

© Scott Foresman 5

Improving Written Answers on Tests

Introduction

Purpose of This Section
This section supplies a bridge between lessons and skills in *Scott Foresman Reading* and the writing skills essential for success on the TCAP Writing Test administered in seventh grade.

The TCAP Writing Test
The TCAP Writing Test requires students to respond to a writing prompt. Students must write an essay on an assigned topic within a specified amount of time. Evaluation is based on a six-point holistic scale. A score of 1 to 6 is assigned to the student's written response, with 6 being the highest.

Contents of This Section
The first page of this section is a rubric for your general use. Customize the rubric to score written responses to any of the writing prompts in this section, or other writing that you assign your students. The remaining pages are divided into units that correspond to the units and their themes in *Scott Foresman Reading*. They give support in preparing your students for the TCAP Writing Test. For each unit, there are eight pages plus a transparency: four teacher support pages and four student pages.

Teacher Support Pages
These include the following: notes on how to use the materials, answers, and fifth-grade writing models with evaluation guides.

Student Support Pages
These blackline masters include the following: a graphic organizer for prewriting, a mini-writing lesson on sentence formation, and a core writing lesson on either content or style.

How to Use This Section
Use the teacher support pages to help you evaluate student writing. Assign all of the student pages. For the Get Started page, which includes a writing prompt and a prewriting organizer, assign the prewriting organizer as an exercise. Then decide whether or not to have students write a response to the writing prompt.

Rubric for General Use

Score   **Description**

6	
5	
4	
3	
2	
1	

Unit 1
Notes to the Teacher

The following materials are to be used with *Faith and Eddie* (page 42) in *Scott Foresman Reading*.

Improve the Writing Sample (Use transparency 1 and the blackline masters on pages 114, 116.)
Show students the transparency, which gives a model of a 2-point writing sample based on the reading selection. You may also wish to photocopy the blackline version of the transparency so students have their own copy. Help students use the Writer's Checklist to evaluate the model and to make corrections and improvements. Write corrections on the transparency. Use the Guide for Writing Transparency 1 on page 112.

Answers to the exercise on page 114
1. It was a sunny afternoon, and I was in my doghouse.
2. I try hard to get away, but he always gets me.
3. Bullo got stuck in the traffic, and I found Ben.

Improve Content (Use the blackline master on page 115.)
Students use elaboration to improve content. Once students have finished this exercise, you may want them to write their own response to the writing prompt on page 113. Remind them to use their graphic organizer and checklist. An example of a 6-point model appears on page 110.

Answers to the exercise on page 115
1. Eddie's charming, amber-colored eyes make him irresistible when he's begging for food.
2. Faith goes to school in a round adobe hut.
3. Eddie knew where Faith's mom was because he saw her funny little red car.
4. Eddie picked up his master's scent and found Faith.
5. Eddie climbed the hill by the spectacular shrines.

Writing Models and Evaluations

Writing Prompt Think of a pet or animal that you know. Write a story or describe something that happens from the animal's point of view. Make your animal as vivid as Eddie.

You might have students write in response to this prompt.

6-Point Score

One morning, on a very hot summer day, Susan and I were playing catch at the park. I'm Susan's dog Waldo and Susan is my best friend. We were having so much fun playing catch when suddenly Susan fainted! I didn't know what to do, so I started going in circuls around her barking for help. No one came, so I ran to an old man sitting on a bench near the dirty, green pond. He seemed not to like dogs because he shooed me away. I got really scared. I was tired out but when I saw three ladies coming my way I ran to them and tried to get them to come to Susan. It worked! They chased after me as I ran to where Susan was.

One of the ladies called 911. The ambulance came to the rescue. At the hospital the doctor called Susan's parents, and they rushed to the hospital. The doctor said Susan only fainted because of the hot sunlight, she was fine now. Susan's parents were very happy. We went in to see her. She was smiling when I came in the door. She ran to me and said, "Thanks a lot Waldo. I'll give you a big doggy treat when we get home!" I was really glad she was okay, but I couldn't wait to get home! "Aarf!"

A 6 paper is OUTSTANDING. It demonstrates a high degree of proficiency in response to the assignment but may have a few minor errors.

An essay in this category:
- is well organized and coherently developed
- clearly explains or illustrates key ideas
- demonstrates syntactic variety
- clearly displays facility in the use of language
- is generally free from errors in mechanics, usage, and sentence structure

5-Point Score

My name is Sly. I am a gecko. That's a lizard. I am the class pet of Mrs. Walsh's third grade class. Today is the first day of school. I'm very excited to see who is in my class this year. I spent the summer with Mrs. Walsh but now I'm back in my old home. The bell is ringing here come the kids! One girl comes right over to me. I lick my eyeballs to see if I can gross her out. That's my best trick. "Ewww!" she says. She laughs and points. Oh good I'm the star!

Now everybody settles down. The teacher tells everybody all the school rules. I know these by heart. I cant wait until the first break. That's when the teacher will show everyone how to feed me my crikets.I just love crikets. I eat them all day if I can. But until then I climb the walls a few times to try to get the kids to look at me. The first day of school is so much fun.

A 5 paper is STRONG. It demonstrates clear proficiency in response to the assignment and may have minor errors.

An essay in this category:
- is generally well organized and coherently developed
- explains or illustrates key ideas
- demonstrates some syntactic variety
- displays facility in the use of language
- is generally free from errors in mechanics, usage, and sentence structure

4-Point Score

Hi! I'm Oliver, but everyone calls me Ollie! Oh no, its my owner Kate! I don't want to play right now!

"Hi, big boy!" Kate is calling and running towards me I'll give her a little bite to let her know who's boss.

"Oh! Mommy, Ollie bit me!" Kate complained.

"He's only nibbling. Let's take him for a walk. He needed a little exersize!" my other master said.

I just wanted to rest. I didn't want to go outside. I didn't want to walk. So I ran under the bed.

"Got ya!" Kate said. "You don't want to be running away! Anyway Mom, when is Becca coming over. She's my favorite cousin."

Kate was very excited to have Becca come over. I was excited also because then Kate would have a friend to play with, and I could rest! I've been up since 3:00 in the morning.

"Ollie, why are you licking my face?" Kate asked.

I was the most happy dog in the world because soon I would be going to sleep.

A 4 paper is COMPETENT. It demonstrates proficiency in response to the assignment.

An essay in this category:
- is adequately organized and developed
- explains or illustrates some of the key ideas
- displays adequate facility in the use of language
- may display some errors in mechanics, usage, or sentence structure

3-Point Score

I like to sit on the windowsill and wait for Andy to come home because the sun feels good on my orange fur. That's right orange fur! I'm a cat. My name is Gumball because Andy says when I was a kitten I curled up in an orange ball. I see Andy coming up the walk. I go to the door to purr and walk around his legs. Andy likes that. Then he will give me my after school snack. He's the best. I like tender vittles. "Oh no! We are out of food." Andy says. That's no good. I meow at him and stomp away to show him I'm mad. But he runs to the store and gets me my vittles and is back in no time. Hes a good owner so I forgive him and purr in his lap. Andy likes that too!

A 3 paper is LIMITED. It demonstrates some degree of proficiency in response to the assignment but is clearly flawed.

An essay in this category reveals one or more of the following weaknesses:
- inadequate organization or development
- inadequate explanation or illustration of key ideas
- limited or inappropriate word choice
- a pattern or accumulation of errors in mechanics, usage, or sentence structure

2-Point Score (See Writing Transparency 1.)

It was a sunny afternoon. I was in my doghouse. It was real peaceful except for one thing, Bullo, the mean nayberhood dog. I try harder to get away. He always gets me. Well anyways my owners are Ben, and ben's parents, Bill and Bernice. "I'm coming for you, Rover, he yelled." I ran for my life to Ben's house. I forgot they've gone out! I started running toward the street. It was probaly rush hour because a lot of cars were on the street. I was lucky. Bullo got stuck in the traffick. I found Ben.

Guide for Writing Transparency 1

A 2 paper is FLAWED. It demonstrates limited proficiency in response to the assignment.

An essay in this category reveals one or more of the following weaknesses:
- weak organization or very little development
- little or no relevant detail
- serious errors in mechanics, usage, sentence structure, or word choice

1-Point Score

I, Elvis one day desided to make movies. I am a fuzy, small, and nice. I just wanted a job. Hamster like to work. Just like people. Elvis will be more gooder then Speelburg Elvis will be the best!

A 1 paper is DEFICIENT. It demonstrates fundamental deficiencies in writing skills.

An essay in this category contains serious and persistent writing errors or is incoherent or is undeveloped.

0.0 is reported accompanied by one of the following codes to indicate a paper could not be scored for one of the following reasons:

A—Blank or Refusal D—Insufficient to Score
B—Illegible E—Predominantly in another language
C—Off Topic

Get Started

Literature Connection *Faith and Eddie* by Patrick Jennings can be found on page 42 of your *Scott Foresman Reading* book. In this story, Faith has to adjust to a new school, and she turns to her dog Eddie for support.

Character Characters are the people or animals in stories. You can learn about them by noticing what they think and do, what they say, what others say about them, and how others treat them.

Prepare to Write Read the prompt. Use the character web below to organize details about the animal in your story.

Writing Prompt Think of a pet or animal that you know. Write a story or describe something that happens from the animal's point of view. Make your animal as vivid as Eddie.

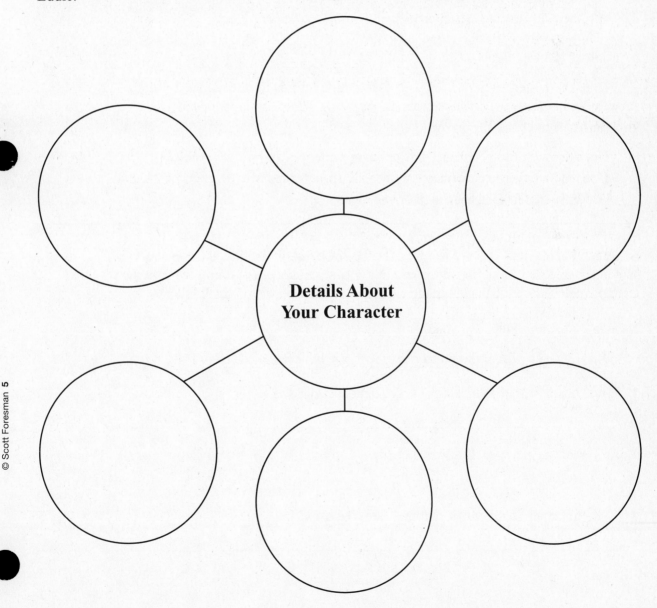

Details About Your Character

Improve the Writing Sample

Use a Writer's Checklist Your teacher will show you a writing transparency. Use the following writer's checklist to think of ways the writing could be improved.

Writer's Checklist

1. Look at the ideas.

___ Does the writer write from an animal's point of view?

___ Does the writer make the animal vivid?

___ Does the writer elaborate by supplying interesting details?

2. Look at the sentences.

___ Could any pairs of short sentences be put together?

___ Are there any sentence fragments?

3. Look at the words.

___ Does the writer use words and details to paint pictures for the reader?

4. Proofread to check for errors.

___ Does the writer use capital letters to begin sentences and proper nouns?

___ Does the writer use punctuation at the end of sentences?

___ Are the verbs in sentences in the same tense?

Sentence Formation Use the word *and* or the word *but* to combine the two short sentences. Replace the period at the end of the first sentence with a comma. See the example below. (Notice that *he* in the new sentence begins with a small letter).

Example: I want to play with Brad. He is sick today. (Use *but.*)

I want to play with Brad, but he is sick today.

1. It was a sunny afternoon. I was in my doghouse. (Use *and.*)

_____

2. I try hard to get away. He always gets me. (Use *but.*)

_____

3. Bullo got stuck in the traffic. I found Ben. (Use *and.*)

_____

© Scott Foresman 5

Improve Content

Elaboration You can elaborate by adding or clarifying details and information. This will help your readers understand or visualize things more clearly.

Directions Improve each sentence by replacing the underlined word or phrase with a phrase that gives more information. Write your new sentence using a phrase from the box. See the example below.

Elaboration Box	
round adobe hut traditional brilliant blue blouses spectacular shrines	charming, amber-colored eyes picked up his master's scent funny little red car

Example: Milagros always wears <u>nice shirts</u>.

_____ Milagros always wears traditional brilliant blue blouses. _____

1. Eddie's <u>best features</u> make him irresistible when he's begging for food.

_____

2. Faith goes to school in a <u>building</u>.

_____

3. Eddie knew where Faith's mom was because he saw her <u>automobile</u>.

_____

4. Eddie <u>went to work</u> and found Faith.

_____

5. Eddie climbed the hill by the <u>graves</u>.

_____

It was a sunny afternoon. I was in my doghouse. It was real peaceful except for one thing, Bullo, the mean nayberhood dog. I try harder to get away. He always gets me. Well anyways my owners are Ben, and ben's parents, Bill and Bernice. "I'm coming for you Rover, he yelled." I ran for my life to Ben's house. I forgot they've gone out! I started running toward the street. It was probaly rush hour because a lot of cars were on the street. I was lucky. Bullo got stuck in the traffick. I found Ben.

© Scott Foresman 5

Unit 2
Notes to the Teacher

The following materials are to be used with *Missing Links* (page 206) in *Scott Foresman Reading*.

Improve the Writing Sample (Use transparency 2 and the blackline masters on pages 122, 124.)

Show students the transparency, which gives a model of a 2-point writing sample based on the reading selection. You may also wish to photocopy the blackline version of the transparency so students have their own copy. Help students use the Writer's Checklist to evaluate the model and to make corrections and improvements. Write corrections on the transparency. Use the Guide for Writing Transparency 2 on page 120.

Answers to the exercise on page 122
1. She was smart. She knew the bread was OK.
2. She is good. She tries to get back home by noon.
3. They like to solve mysteries. I don't.

Improve Style (Use the blackline master on page 123.)

Students use vivid words to improve style. Once students have finished this exercise, you may want them to write their own response to the writing prompt on page 121. Remind them to use their graphic organizer and checklist. An example of a 6-point model appears on page 118.

Answers to the exercise on page 123
1. Sherlock looked at the men's tie pins and cuff links.
2. The glass display case held beautiful rings.
3. Salespeople were racing back and forth.
4. Amanda and Sherlock looked at the jewelry salesman.
5. The salesman stuffed the ties in the case.
6. He was peering into the shattered display case.

Writing Models and Evaluations

Writing Prompt Write a composition in which you draw some conclusions about Amanda and Sherlock. Choose three words to describe each character and explain your choices. Tell whether or not you would want them for friends.

You might have students write in response to this prompt.

6-Point Score

Amanda is observant, curious, and intelligent. She is careful to observe the baker and the jewelry salesman before, during, and after the crime. She is curious about what she notices. And uses her intelligence to reach accurate conclusions about what happened. Because of these three characteristics, Amanda solves the crime.

Sherlock, is also curious, observant, and intelligent. Observant Sherlock carries a magnifying glass. He observes details like the stain on the salesman's tie and checks for fingerprints with his magnifying glass. He uses his intelligence to think about what he sees, like the door marked "sprinkler control room," to solve the crime that took place.

I would like to be friends with Amanda and Sherlock. It would be entertaining and exciting to solve crimes in our city! We could start our own detectave agency.

A 6 paper is OUTSTANDING. It demonstrates a high degree of proficiency in response to the assignment but may have a few minor errors.

An essay in this category:
- is well organized and coherently developed
- clearly explains or illustrates key ideas
- demonstrates syntactic variety
- clearly displays facility in the use of language
- is generally free from errors in mechanics, usage, and sentence structure

5-Point Score

Amanda is smart, quick and nice. She is smart because she notices the clues that solve the case in the end. She puts all the clues together as soon as she sees the sapphire ring on the Baker's hand. That's quick thinking. She is also nice. She is always thinking about other people first. She reminds her brother to shop for their dad and she feels bad for the jewelry man before she finds out he's the thief.

Sherlock is smart too because he notices the clues. He's also suspicous. He carries around a magnifying glass like he always thinks something will go wrong. He examines the man's tie because he doesn't believe that it's ketchup. He is also annoying how he's always inspecting everything.

They would be great friends because they always solve mysteries. I like how they work as a team and get along. It's good to have smart friends around in case you need something figured out.

A 5 paper is STRONG. It demonstrates clear proficiency in response to the assignment and may have minor errors.

An essay in this category:
- is generally well organized and coherently developed
- explains or illustrates key ideas
- demonstrates some syntactic variety
- displays facility in the use of language
- is generally free from errors in mechanics, usage, and sentence structure

4-Point Score

I know that Amanda is very clever. Because she knew that it wasn't plaster dust but that it was flour instead. She also figures out that the baker stole the jewelry. Amanda is confident, she knew she could solve the mystery. Amanda is smart because she is suspicious about the baker.

Sherlock is determined because he figures out the mystery before the police do. He is a little wild because he is always running around and using his magnifing glass and looking for prints. He is smart because he figures out the stain on the tie is blood, not ketchup.

I'd like them both as friends and think it will be fun to go with them and solve mysterys and have adventures and be detectives. We could become famous.

A 4 paper is COMPETENT. It demonstrates proficiency in response to the assignment.

An essay in this category:
- is adequately organized and developed
- explains or illustrates some of the key ideas
- displays adequate facility in the use of language
- may display some errors in mechanics, usage, or sentence structure

3-Point Score

Amanda and Sherlock are amazing! I could never have solved the mystry. I had to look back at the pictures but they figured it out all on their own. They put together all the clues so fast. They are also suspisious. They know something is not right with the jewlery man and the baker. They don't seem to believe their stories. They are wise too. They seem to be able to figure out things before the grownups or the police or anybody. They must have done this before which makes them wise about crime. I would want Amanda and Sherlock to be my friends so no one could get away with stealing anything from me I bet they'd teach me some crime solving tricks.

A 3 paper is LIMITED. It demonstrates some degree of proficiency in response to the assignment but is clearly flawed.

An essay in this category reveals one or more of the following weaknesses:
- inadequate organization or development
- inadequate explanation or illustration of key ideas
- limited or inappropriate word choice
- a pattern or accumulation of errors in mechanics, usage, or sentence structure

© Scott Foresman 5

2-Point Score (See Writing Transparency 2.)

Amanda is smart, serious, and good. She was smart, she knew the bread was OK. She is serious when she solves the mystery. She was good, she tries to get back home by noon. Sherlock is hungary, nice, and smart. He was hungary when he wants a choclate thing. He is nice sometimes. He is smart when he solves the mystery. Amanda and Sherlock are more nice then lots of kids, but I wouldnt want to be freinds. They like to solve mysteries, I don't.

Guide for Writing Transparency 2

A 2 paper is FLAWED. It demonstrates limited proficiency in response to the assignment.

An essay in this category reveals one or more of the following weaknesses:
- weak organization or very little development
- little or no relevant detail
- serious errors in mechanics, usage, sentence structure, or word choice

1-Point Score

Amanda is nice. She brung Sherlock to the store and is helpfol to do what she have to. Sherlock likes to find clews and be smart and he is more littler then Amanda because she is the big sister.

A 1 paper is DEFICIENT. It demonstrates fundamental deficiencies in writing skills.

An essay in this category contains serious and persistent writing errors or is incoherent or is undeveloped.

0.0 is reported accompanied by one of the following codes to indicate a paper could not be scored for one of the following reasons:

A—Blank or Refusal
B—Illegible
C—Off Topic

D—Insufficient to Score
E—Predominantly in another language

Get Started

Literature Connection *Missing Links* by Andrew Bromberg can be found on page 206 of your *Scott Foresman Reading* book. In this story, a theft occurs while Amanda and Sherlock are shopping.

Drawing Conclusions When you form opinions based on facts and details, you are drawing conclusions. Think logically as you use clues from what you've read and your own knowledge and experience.

Prepare to Write Read the prompt. Use the charts below to draw your conclusions about Amanda and Sherlock.

Writing Prompt Write a composition in which you draw some conclusions about Amanda and Sherlock. Choose three words to describe each character and explain your choices. Tell whether or not you would want them for friends.

Amanda's Character Traits   **Clues from the Story**

1. _____ → _____

2. _____ → _____

3. _____ → _____

Sherlock's Character Traits   **Clues from the Story**

1. _____ → _____

2. _____ → _____

3. _____ → _____

Improve the Writing Sample

Use a Writer's Checklist Your teacher will show you a writing transparency. Use the following writer's checklist to think of ways the writing could be improved.

Writer's Checklist

1. Look at the ideas.

___ Does the writer draw logical conclusions about Amanda and Sherlock?

___ Does the writer tell whether he or she would like either character for a friend?

___ Does the writer elaborate by supplying interesting details?

2. Look at the sentences.

___ Are there any run-on sentences?

___ Are there any sentence fragments?

3. Look at the words.

___ Does the writer use words and details to paint pictures for the reader?

4. Proofread to check for errors.

___ Does the writer use capital letters to begin sentences and proper nouns?

___ Does the writer use punctuation at the end of sentences?

___ Are all words spelled correctly?

Sentence Formation Turn each run-on sentence into two separate sentences. For each item, replace the comma with a period. Begin the first word of the new sentence with a capital letter. See the example below.

Example: Amanda is older than Sherlock, she seems smarter too.

Amanda is older than Sherlock. She seems smarter too.

1. She was smart, she knew the bread was OK.

_____

2. She is good, she tries to get back home by noon.

_____

3. They like to solve mysteries, I don't.

_____

© Scott Foresman 5

Improve Style

Vivid Words Choose vivid words to keep your writing interesting. Remember, you want to hold your reader's attention!

Directions Rewrite each sentence by replacing the underlined word or words with vocabulary that is more vivid. Use words from the box.

Vocabulary Box	
computer games glass display case shattered jewelry salesman	men's tie pins and cuff links stuffed racing back and forth

Example: Sherlock plays with stuff.

_____ Sherlock plays with computer games. _____

1. Sherlock looked at the jewelry.

_____

2. The counter held beautiful rings.

_____

3. Salespeople were running.

_____

4. Amanda and Sherlock looked at the man.

_____

5. The salesman put the ties in the case.

_____

6. He was peering into the broken display case.

_____

Amanda is smart, serious, and good. She was smart, she knew the bread was OK. She is serious when she solves the mystery. She was good, she tries to get back home by noon. Sherlock is hungary, nice, and smart. He was hungary when he wants a choclate thing. He is nice sometimes. He is smart when he solves the mystery. Amanda and Sherlock are more nice then lots of kids, but I wouldnt want to be freinds. They like to solve mysteries, I don't.

Unit 3
Notes to the Teacher

The following materials are to be used with *Babe to the Rescue* (page 302) in *Scott Foresman Reading*.

Improve the Writing Sample (Use transparency 3 and the blackline masters on pages 130, 132.)
Show students the transparency, which gives a model of a 2-point writing sample based on the reading selection. You may also wish to photocopy the blackline version of the transparency so students have their own copy. Help students use the Writer's Checklist to evaluate the model and to make corrections and improvements. Write corrections on the transparency. Use the Guide for Writing Transparency 3 on page 128.

Answers to the exercise on page 130
1. I was swimming and practicing my strokes.
2. He saw the shark near him and waved madly.
3. We swam back to shore and never went to Diamond Beach again.

Improve Content (Use the blackline master on page 131.)
Students use organization and unity to improve content. Once students have finished this exercise, you may want them to write their own response to the writing prompt on page 129. Remind them to use their graphic organizer and checklist. An example of a 6-point model appears on page 126.

Answers to the exercise on page 131
The edited paragraph:
   Babe decided to visit a flock of sheep, and his visit turned into quite an adventure! Babe went up the hill to where the sheep were, but he didn't see a single sheep. Then Babe saw the whole flock of sheep galloping toward him. Leading the sheep were two dogs. Babe saw his friend Ma and asked her what was going on. Ma explained to Babe that there were sheep stealers on top of the hill. Babe decided that he had to save the sheep from the sheep stealers. Babe's unexpected appearance created chaos. All of the noise drove the sheep stealers away. Babe was a hero!

Writing Models and Evaluations

6-Point Score

I came to the rescue for a six-year-old boy at camp last summer. One day after I got to camp, I put my bag down and went to go play tennis with my friend Brett, who is a really good player. On my way over to the tennis court, I noticed a big bully being mean to a little red-haired boy on my bus named Seth. Seth was playing with a bouncy ball, and the big bully grabbed the ball away and threw it into the baseball field. Seth started to cry. I felt sorry for him and asked him if he was okay. He said that the bully threw his ball into the field just to be mean.

I told Seth that I would get his ball back and bring it to him tomorrow. I also made Seth my bus buddy and walked with him to meet his group. I talked to Seth's bully and worked it out. I am older then the bully, so he listened to me. I looked him straight in the eye, so he knew I meant business. I told the bully that Seth was my buddy, and if he picked on him, I would know about it. I don't think he will bother Seth again! Seth was so happy that he gave me some of his baseball cards!

A 6 paper is OUTSTANDING. It demonstrates a high degree of proficiency in response to the assignment but may have a few minor errors.

An essay in this category:
• is well organized and coherently developed
• clearly explains or illustrates key ideas
• demonstrates syntactic variety
• clearly displays facility in the use of language
• is generally free from errors in mechanics, usage, and sentence structure

5-Point Score

I helped my little brother, had a good idea and made him happy all at once on Halloween! My brother Brendan left his hairy tarantula costume at school. He didn't remember until it was too late and the school was all locked up for the night. He was so sad and kept crying. I was sad too. That costume took a long time to make and we only had a little time before trick or treat started. Suddenly I had an idea I knew he wanted to be a bug so I thought "Why not be a bee? It's easy!" Brendan smiled and thought that was a good idea.

First we dressed him in all black and put a pillow under his shirt. He looked so chubby and cute. Then I took yellow masking tape and gave him stripes all around. Then I took a tube and rapped it in tinfoil and strapped it on for a stinger. Last I made antena out of an old headband. He looked great and he got lots of candy.

A 5 paper is STRONG. It demonstrates clear proficiency in response to the assignment and may have minor errors.

An essay in this category:
- is generally well organized and coherently developed
- explains or illustrates key ideas
- demonstrates some syntactic variety
- displays facility in the use of language
- is generally free from errors in mechanics, usage, and sentence structure

4-Point Score

I came to the rescue when my sister Beth was stuck on our swing sets top bar. My mom and dad weren't home, so I had to help her myself. She was really scared. Me too. I told her to hold on tight and that it would be okay. I went to get my little brother Jordan, who was in the house. I had a plan to get her down.

First, I climed the tall slide to get onto the small red bar. From there, I got on the big yellow bar. Next I held my breath and scoted over to Beth. I brought her to the low bar, and Jordan took her off the low bar. I could tell she was heavy for him, but he held her tight. He didn't drop her. From the low bar, she went down the slide with a loud cheer. Now that is how I came to the rescue.

A 4 paper is COMPETENT. It demonstrates proficiency in response to the assignment.

An essay in this category:
- is adequately organized and developed
- explains or illustrates some of the key ideas
- displays adequate facility in the use of language
- may display some errors in mechanics, usage, or sentence structure

3-Point Score

I was to the rescue last year on summer vacation. Me and my buddies were riding our bikes on the dirt road by the lake. Everybody does but sometimes turns are trickie because your wheels go sideways. My buddy Tommy was right a head of me and he totally spun out and crashed. Oh man! we said because it looked like it hurt. Turned out he got four stitches in one knee. Tommys knees were bloody and covered in dirt, but he was okay. I took off my shirt and wiped off his knees and pressed on the cuts. I told my other buddy to wait there with Tommy and press on his cuts. I rode to his house and got his dad and we drove back to pick him up.

A 3 paper is LIMITED. It demonstrates some degree of proficiency in response to the assignment but is clearly flawed.

An essay in this category reveals one or more of the following weaknesses:
- inadequate organization or development
- inadequate explanation or illustration of key ideas
- limited or inappropriate word choice
- a pattern or accumulation of errors in mechanics, usage, or sentence structure

2-Point Score (See Writing Transparency 3.)

One day I was on the beach. I was swimming. I was practicing my strokes. Swimming at Diamond Beach in sunny July weather. All was going well until a shark decided to pop up and everybody run out of the Ocean. Ecept for my younger brother Bradley. He saw the shark near him. He waved madly. I had to save him. So I jump in the water strugled to get Bradley away from the shark and than I did. We swam back to shore. We never went to Diamond Beach again.

Guide for Writing Transparency 3

A 2 paper is FLAWED. It demonstrates limited proficiency in response to the assignment.

An essay in this category reveals one or more of the following weaknesses:
- weak organization or very little development
- little or no relevant detail
- serious errors in mechanics, usage, sentence structure, or word choice

1-Point Score

When I came to the reskue. It was at my baskitbal game. In the JCC leage. It wasnt the Champion Chip. We need to get 1 basket it was the 2nd game. There were 3 seconds left. We got the ball, shot, and made it. We won the game.

A 1 paper is DEFICIENT. It demonstrates fundamental deficiencies in writing skills.

An essay in this category contains serious and persistent writing errors or is incoherent or is undeveloped.

0.0 is reported accompanied by one of the following codes to indicate a paper could not be scored for one of the following reasons:

A—Blank or Refusal   D—Insufficient to Score
B—Illegible   E—Predominantly in another language
C—Off Topic

Get Started

Literature Connection *Babe to the Rescue* by Dick King-Smith can be found on page 302 of your *Scott Foresman Reading* book. In this story, Babe, the pig, saves a flock of sheep from being stolen.

Summarizing Summarizing means telling just the central ideas of an article or the plot of a story. A good summary is brief and doesn't include unnecessary details, repeated words or thoughts, or unimportant ideas.

Prepare to Write Read the prompt. Use the chart below to organize your story about how you came to someone's rescue.

Writing Prompt Think about a time when you came to the rescue. It could be when you helped someone, had a good idea, or made someone happy. Write a summary of what happened.

Beginning:

Middle:

End:

Improve the Writing Sample

Use a Writer's Checklist Your teacher will show you a writing transparency. Use the following writer's checklist to think of ways the writing could be improved.

Writer's Checklist

1. Look at the ideas.

___ Does the writer stick to the central idea by telling a personal story?
___ Does the writer summarize?
___ Does the writer elaborate by supplying necessary details?

2. Look at the sentences.

___ Could any pairs of short sentences be put together?
___ Are there any sentence fragments?

3. Look at the words.

___ Does the writer use words and details to paint pictures for the reader?

4. Proofread to check for errors.

___ Does the writer use capital letters to begin sentences and proper nouns?
___ Does the writer use punctuation at the end of sentences?
___ Are the verbs in sentences in the same tense?

Sentence Formation Combine the two short sentences. In the new sentence, replace the period and any unnecessary words with the word *and*. See the example below. (Notice that *we* is omitted in the new sentence).

Example: We went swimming. We ate lunch.

_____We went swimming and ate lunch._____

1. I was swimming. I was practicing my strokes.

_____

2. He saw the shark near him. He waved madly.

_____

3. We swam back to shore. We never went to Diamond Beach again.

_____

© Scott Foresman 5

Improve Content

Organization and Unity When you write, make sure every sentence says something about the central idea, or main idea. Check that sentences are in the right order.

Directions Read the paragraph below. The first sentence tells the central idea.
1. Draw a line through two sentences that do not tell about the central idea.
2. Find one sentence that is out of order and draw an arrow to where it should go.
3. Write the new paragraph on the lines below.

Babe decided to visit a flock of sheep, and his visit turned into quite an adventure! Babe went up the hill to where the sheep were, but he didn't see a single sheep. Then Babe saw the whole flock of sheep galloping toward him. On market day, his boss and mum went into town. Leading the sheep were two dogs. Ma explained to Babe that there were sheep stealers on top of the hill. Babe saw his friend Ma and asked her what was going on. Babe decided that he had to save the sheep from the sheep stealers. Babe's unexpected appearance created chaos. Farmer Hogget liked Babe. All of the noise drove the sheep stealers away. Babe was a hero!

_____

_____

_____

_____

_____

_____

_____

_____

_____

_____

One day I was on the beach. I was swimming. I was practicing my strokes. Swimming at Diamond Beach in sunny July weather. All was going well until a shark decided to pop up and everybody run out of the Ocean. Ecept for my younger brother Bradley. He saw the shark near him. He waved madly. I had to save him. So I jump in the water strugled to get Bradley away from the shark and than I did. We swam back to shore. We never went to Diamond Beach again.

Unit 4
Notes to the Teacher

The following materials are to be used with *The Night Alone* (page 372) in *Scott Foresman Reading*.

Improve the Writing Sample (Use transparency 4 and the blackline masters on pages 138, 140.)
Show students the transparency, which gives a model of a 2-point writing sample based on the reading selection. You may also wish to photocopy the blackline version of the transparency so students have their own copy. Help students use the Writer's Checklist to evaluate the model and to make corrections and improvements. Write corrections on the transparency. Use the Guide for Writing Transparency 4 on page 136.

Answers to the exercise on page 138
1. I am alone at night in a tent.
2. All I can see is the dark night.
3. I am still in my room in bed.

Improve Content (Use the blackline master on page 139.)
Students use elaboration to improve content. Once students have finished this exercise, you may want them to write their own response to the writing prompt on page 137. Remind them to use their graphic organizer and checklist. An example of a 6-point model appears on page 134.

Answers to the exercise on page 139
1. The hissing, popping, and crackling noises of the fire were familiar to him.
2. Ohkwa'ri noticed the coiled rattlesnake in the path.
3. She placed the ripe strawberries in a basket for him.
4. That night, Ohkwa'ri saw two small shadows moving outside his door.
5. He remembered the story Uncle Big Tree told about the two young men.
6. Then he opened the drawstring of the pouch and shook out its contents into his lap.

Writing Models and Evaluations

Writing Prompt Imagine you are alone in a strange place at night. Suddenly there is an odd noise. In two paragraphs, describe that place, predict what happens next, and describe what you feel and do.

You might have students write in response to this prompt.

6-Point Score

One night when I was spending the night in an old, dark, drafty castle, I heard a very strange noise. I only had two candles for light. There weren't any other lights in the house to see what was going on. The sound was scary and frightening, but not very loud. It sounded like scratching. Maybe it was a mouse or the wind blowing something around. It sounded like it was in the room next to mine. I decided to get out of the huge canopie bed and go and see what the noise was. Even though I was scared, I wanted to see what was happening.

I got up from the bed. I took one of the candles with me so I could see. When I was walking to the door, I heard another noise from next door. I kept walking even though I was scared. I thought that somebody had broken into the castle to steal jewelry. When I got to the door of the room, I stopped. Then, I slowly opened the door to peek inside. I heard a crashing noise. All of a sudden a cat ran right past me out of the dark room and down the hall! It must have been scared too. Like I was.

A 6 paper is OUTSTANDING. It demonstrates a high degree of proficiency in response to the assignment but may have a few minor errors.
An essay in this category:
- is well organized and coherently developed
- clearly explains or illustrates key ideas
- demonstrates syntactic variety
- clearly displays facility in the use of language
- is generally free from errors in mechanics, usage, and sentence structure

5-Point Score

One night I was trapped in haunted house. It was creepy and spooky. I was terrified so I turned on all the lights. I didn't want anything to happen to me. Then I hear howling coming from the second floor. "What was that!" I knew it was the ghost that haunted that place. Then I heard a bang!

I creeped up the creeky stairs one at a time. The howls are louder and sound like they are saying "Whooo are youuuu?" It's like a movie I saw with my big sister once. I freeze on the stairs because I don't know what to do. Then I hear the bang again and I see that theres a loose shutter on a window. Then I realise it was only the wind. After that I was okay until the sun came up and I escaped.

A 5 paper is STRONG. It demonstrates clear proficiency in response to the assignment and may have minor errors.

An essay in this category:
- is generally well organized and coherently developed
- explains or illustrates key ideas
- demonstrates some syntactic variety
- displays facility in the use of language
- is generally free from errors in mechanics, usage, and sentence structure

4-Point Score

I'm in a deep deep backwoods in a small dark log cabin. Before I go to bed, I hear a soft thump on the door. I open the door, but there is no one or thing there. I close the door, but I hear the noise again even louder. I open the door again, but there is nothing there. I think that it must have been the wind, or a tree branch.

A few minutes later, I hear scratching. I thought it was a raccoon, but when I go outside to try to make it leave, I am complitly scared. It was a big, brown bear, not a raccoon. I go into the cabin. I grab the leftover rabbit meat. Then, I threw it far away. The bear goes after the meat. I wate outside for about an hour and go to bed. I lock the door so the bear won't get in.

A 4 paper is COMPETENT. It demonstrates proficiency in response to the assignment.

An essay in this category:
- is adequately organized and developed
- explains or illustrates some of the key ideas
- displays adequate facility in the use of language
- may display some errors in mechanics, usage, or sentence structure

3-Point Score

It was a dark night and I had to go up into the attic to get my dad's toolbox. I never go up there. All of a sudden I hear a THUMP THUMP. I don't know what it is so I walk closer to get a look and point my flash light. That's when I see the shado moving around. What can it be? Then I hear a squeeking and it sounds like an animal all of a sudden this ugly vampire bat comes flying at me! I hit the floor and start yelling at the top of my lung sand then my dad comes and opens the window and bye bye bat.

A 3 paper is LIMITED. It demonstrates some degree of proficiency in response to the assignment but is clearly flawed.

An essay in this category reveals one or more of the following weaknesses:
- inadequate organization or development
- inadequate explanation or illustration of key ideas
- limited or inappropriate word choice
- a pattern or accumulation of errors in mechanics, usage, or sentence structure

© Scott Foresman 5

2-Point Score (See Writing Transparency 4.)

> I am alone at night. In a tent. All of a suden I heard a thumping sound coming from outside. I look outside to see what creture it is, but there was nothing there. All that I see. Is the dark night. I go back into my tent I take one last look around outside to see where I am and I get grabbed around the neck! Then I look around and realize that it was all a dream. I am still in my room. In bed. I realize that I am still in my pijamas and decide to go back to sleep.

Guide for Writing Transparency 4

A 2 paper is FLAWED. It demonstrates limited proficiency in response to the assignment.

An essay in this category reveals one or more of the following weaknesses:

- weak organization or very little development
- little or no relevant detail
- serious errors in mechanics, usage, sentence structure, or word choice

1-Point Score

> I was in a tent. its cold and scared. I herd the noise, and I got scareder. When I herd it. It is lowd and fritened me. When I herd it. I run away from the noise away to a house. Where I was safe. Not like the tent. It was better then.

A 1 paper is DEFICIENT. It demonstrates fundamental deficiencies in writing skills.

An essay in this category contains serious and persistent writing errors or is incoherent or is undeveloped.

0.0 is reported accompanied by one of the following codes to indicate a paper could not be scored for one of the following reasons:

A—Blank or Refusal	D—Insufficient to Score
B—Illegible	E—Predominantly in another language
C—Off Topic	

Get Started

Literature Connection *The Night Alone* by Joseph Bruchac can be found on page 372 of your *Scott Foresman Reading* book. In this story, Ohkwa'ri, a Native American boy, spends the night alone in his new lodge.

Predicting When you give a statement about what you think might happen next in a story, you are making a prediction. You can make predictions based on what you know and what has already happened in a story.

Prepare to Write Imagine that you, like Ohkwa'ri, were spending a night alone. Read the prompt. Use the chart below to organize your ideas.

Writing Prompt Imagine you are alone in a strange place at night. Suddenly there is an odd noise. In two paragraphs, describe the place and the noise, predict what happens next, and describe what you feel and do.

Description of the Place and Noise

⇩

Predictions

Improve the Writing Sample

Use a Writer's Checklist Your teacher will show you a writing transparency. Use the following writer's checklist to think of ways the writing could be improved.

Writer's Checklist

1. Look at the ideas.

___ Does the writer stick to the central idea by describing his/her night alone?

___ Does the writer include predictions?

___ Does the writer elaborate by supplying interesting details?

2. Look at the sentences.

___ Could any pairs of short sentences be put together?

___ Are there any sentence fragments?

3. Look at the words.

___ Does the writer use words and details to paint pictures for the reader?

4. Proofread to check for errors.

___ Does the writer use capital letters to begin sentences and proper nouns?

___ Does the writer use punctuation at the end of sentences?

___ Are the verb forms and tenses correct?

Sentence Formation A complete sentence must have a subject and a predicate. Combine each sentence fragment with the sentence that precedes it. See the example below.

Example: I turn around. When I hear a sound.

_____ I turn around when I hear a sound. _____

1. I am alone at night. In a tent.

_____

2. All I can see is. The dark night.

_____

3. I am still in my room. In bed.

_____

Improve Content

Elaboration You can elaborate by adding or clarifying details and information. This will help your readers understand or visualize things more clearly.

Directions Improve each sentence by replacing the underlined word or phrase with a phrase that gives more information. Write your new sentence using a phrase from the box.

Elaboration Box	
drawstring of the pouch two small shadows ripe strawberries little wooden canoe	hissing, popping, and crackling noises Uncle Big Tree coiled rattlesnake

Example: He walked to the river and climbed into the <u>boat</u>.

He walked to the river and climbed into the little wooden canoe.

1. The <u>sounds</u> of the fire were familiar to him.

2. Ohkwa'ri noticed the <u>creature</u> in the path.

3. She placed the <u>fruit</u> in a basket for him.

4. That night, Ohkwa'ri saw <u>things</u> moving outside his door.

5. He remembered the story <u>the man</u> told about the two young men.

6. Then he opened the <u>bag</u> and shook out its contents into his lap.

I am alone at night. In a tent. All of a suden I heard a thumping sound coming from outside. I look outside to see what creture it is, but there was nothing there. All that I see. Is the dark night. I go back into my tent I take one last look around outside to see where I am and I get grabbed around the neck! Then I look around and realize that it was all a dream. I am still in my room. In bed. I realize that I am still in my pijamas and decide to go back to sleep.

Unit 5
Notes to the Teacher

The following materials are to be used with *The Long Path to Freedom* (page 468) in *Scott Foresman Reading*.

Improve the Writing Sample (Use transparency 5 and the blackline masters on pages 146, 148.)

Show students the transparency, which gives a model of a 2-point writing sample based on the reading selection. You may also wish to photocopy the blackline version of the transparency so students have their own copy. Help students use the Writer's Checklist to evaluate the model and to make corrections and improvements. Write corrections on the transparency. Use the Guide for Writing Transparency 5 on page 144.

Answers to the exercise on page 146
1. Harriet Tubman was a slave. She didn't want to go to the South.
2. The noises scared her brothers. They probably thought there were lots of big, fierce animals in that forest.
3. Harriet wanted to keep going. They wouldn't let her.

Improve Style (Use the blackline master on page 147.)

Students use vivid words to improve style. Once students have finished this exercise, you may want them to write their own response to the writing prompt on page 145. Remind them to use their graphic organizer and checklist. An example of a 6-point model appears on page 142.

Answers to the exercise on page 147
1. Harriet thought she was free, but then she was snatched up by another slave owner.
2. Harriet wore a bandanna to hide the scar on her forehead.
3. The noise of the horses snuffling and stomping woke her.
4. Wading through streams made it harder for bloodhounds to pick up her scent.
5. The man in the graveyard was muttering to himself.
6. No one guessed that the woman in the elegant clothes was a runaway slave.

© Scott Foresman 5

Writing Models and Evaluations

Writing Prompt The first time that Harriet Tubman tries to escape is described on page 472. Write several paragraphs in which you paraphrase, or tell in your own words, what happens in this passage.

> You might have students write in response to this prompt.

6-Point Score

      Harriet always wanted to escape from the plantation where she worked. But she had spells that made her fall asleep, and she had a nasty scar on her head that was pretty conspikuous and made people notice her! So it was pretty hard.

      But one day Harriet heard the news that a slave trader from the South was coming. She knew that she and her brothers would probably be sold to him. She decided then and there that they had to escape that very night.

      Once her husband was asleep, Harriet and her brothers took off running through the woods. But every time they heard a noise, like a owl or a frog, her brothers nearly hyperventalated! This slowed them down a lot.

      Harriet tried to keep her brothers moving. But they didn't move very fast or very quietly, neither. Finally, her brothers stopped and said they were going back, and she was going with them. Harriet said she wouldn't. But her brothers wouldn't listen and dragged her back with them, even though she fought like a tiger.

A 6 paper is OUTSTANDING. It demonstrates a high degree of proficiency in response to the assignment but may have a few minor errors.

An essay in this category:
- is well organized and coherently developed
- clearly explains or illustrates key ideas
- demonstrates syntactic variety
- clearly displays facility in the use of language
- is generally free from errors in mechanics, usage, and sentence structure

5-Point Score

      Harriet Tubman had to exscape from her plantation because she was going to be sold to the south. She was very scared because she might fall asleep. Or be noticed. But she still knew that she had to try because nothing was worse than the chain gang.

      She waited untill dark to leave. She got her brothers and they all left very quiet. They could not run or they would wake everybody up. Harriet knew the woods and the animals that lived there so she led the way. Her brothers were way too frightened. They couldn't go on and made Harriet turn back. She fought tooth and nail but it didn't matter. Harriet would have to exscape another time.

A 5 paper is STRONG. It demonstrates clear proficiency in response to the assignment and may have minor errors.

An essay in this category:
- is generally well organized and coherently developed
- explains or illustrates key ideas
- demonstrates some syntactic variety
- displays facility in the use of language
- is generally free from errors in mechanics, usage, and sentence structure

4-Point Score

Harriet didn't want to be taken to the South by the people who bought slaves, they were coming that day, so she decided that her and her brothers should escape the plantation that night. And run to freedom. When her husband was sound asleep, she woke up her brothers and whispered, "Follow me!" She led them into woods that were as dark as a coal mine. Her brothers jumped every time they heard any little thing, like a hooting owl or a croaking frog! Finally they just quit following her and said, "We're going back." Harriet said, "No you're not!" "We have to keep going!" But her brothers were too scared. Since there were three of them and only one of Harriet, they made her go back. She fought really hard not to.

A 4 paper is COMPETENT. It demonstrates proficiency in response to the assignment.

An essay in this category:
- is adequately organized and developed
- explains or illustrates some of the key ideas
- displays adequate facility in the use of language
- may display some errors in mechanics, usage, or sentence structure

3-Point Score

Harriet was a brave lady. She wanted to escape from the people in the south. She had to leave in the middle of the dark night so she wouldn't get caught. Her brothers too. They all left quiet as mice so they wouldnt stomp. The frogs and owls were scareing her brothers. Harriet tried to get everyone to keep going but they wanted to go back because they were afraid and said it was riskful. I wanted Harriet to keep going! Her brothers grabbed her and made her go back. I was angry at them but Harriet tried again later and made it.

A 3 paper is LIMITED. It demonstrates some degree of proficiency in response to the assignment but is clearly flawed.

An essay in this category reveals one or more of the following weaknesses:
- inadequate organization or development
- inadequate explanation or illustration of key ideas
- limited or inappropriate word choice
- a pattern or accumulation of errors in mechanics, usage, or sentence structure

2-Point Score (See Writing Transparency 5.)

Harriet Tubman was a slave, she didnt want to go to the South. But some mens were coming to take her to the south. She and her brother's runned away into the forest. I think they should just say they wont go to the south. The noises scared her brothers, they probably thought there was lots of big, feerce animals in that forest. But really only owls and frogs. They said their going back home. Harriet wanted to keep going, they wouldn't let her. Finully, she goes back to.

Guide for Writing Transparency 5

A 2 paper is FLAWED. It demonstrates limited proficiency in response to the assignment.

An essay in this category reveals one or more of the following weaknesses:
- weak organization or very little development
- little or no relevant detail
- serious errors in mechanics, usage, sentence structure, or word choice

1-Point Score

Poor Hariet. These bad guys wants to take her to the south. Ther was three brothers ther was only one sister. She don't want to be a slave and she tries to run away her brothers mak her come back. I think she should get to do what she wants. I wonder what happened to her husband.

A 1 paper is DEFICIENT. It demonstrates fundamental deficiencies in writing skills.

An essay in this category contains serious and persistent writing errors or is incoherent or is undeveloped.

0.0 is reported accompanied by one of the following codes to indicate a paper could not be scored for one of the following reasons:

A—Blank or Refusal   D—Insufficient to Score
B—Illegible   E—Predominantly in another language
C—Off Topic

Get Started

Literature Connection *The Long Path to Freedom* from *The Story of Harriet Tubman* by Kate McMullan begins on page 468 of your *Scott Foresman Reading* book. This historical fiction selection gives a glimpse of heroism in the face of danger.

Paraphrasing Paraphrasing is explaining something in your own words. When paraphrasing, it is important to keep the author's meaning and not add your own opinions. Paraphrasing helps you remember ideas better.

Prepare to Write Read the prompt. Use the chart below to organize your ideas about the passage that you will paraphrase.

Writing Prompt The first time that Harriet Tubman tries to escape is described on page 472. Write several paragraphs in which you paraphrase, or tell in your own words, what happens in this passage.

Beginning:

Middle:

End:

Improve the Writing Sample

Use a Writer's Checklist Your teacher will show you a writing transparency. Use the following writer's checklist to think of ways the writing could be improved.

Writer's Checklist

1. Look at the ideas.

___ Does the writer include all the important ideas of the passage as he or she paraphrases?

___ Does the writer use only information from the assigned passage?

___ Does the writer elaborate by supplying interesting details?

2. Look at the sentences.

___ Does the writer run together sentences that should stand alone?

___ Does the writer use a variety of sentence types in the paraphrased material?

___ Does the writer use punctuation at the end of sentences?

3. Look at the words.

___ Does the writer use vivid words and details to paint pictures for the reader?

4. Proofread to check for errors.

___ Does the writer use capital letters to begin sentences and proper nouns?

___ Does the writer use the same verb tense throughout?

___ Are all the words spelled correctly?

Sentence Formation Look for sentences that run together. Replace the commas with periods to separate them. Remember to capitalize the first word of the new second sentence.

Example: Harriet's brothers were afraid, they wanted to run back home.

___Harriet's brothers were afraid. They wanted to run back home.___

1. Harriet Tubman was a slave, she didn't want to go to the South.

_____

2. The noises scared her brothers, they probably thought there were lots of big, fierce animals in that forest.

_____

3. Harriet wanted to keep going, they wouldn't let her.

_____

Improve Style

Vivid Words Choose vivid words to keep your writing interesting. Remember, you want to hold your reader's attention!

Directions Rewrite each sentence by replacing the underlined word with vocabulary that is more vivid. Use words from the box.

Vocabulary Box	
snatched up plantation elegant bandanna	bloodhounds muttering snuffling

Example: Harriet dreamed of leaving the <u>farm</u> and being free.

        Harriet dreamed of leaving the plantation and being free.

1. Harriet thought she was free, but then she was <u>taken</u> by another slave owner.

    _____

2. Harriet wore a <u>scarf</u> to hide the scar on her forehead.

    _____

3. The noise of the horses <u>breathing</u> and stomping woke her.

    _____

4. Wading through streams made it harder for <u>dogs</u> to pick up her scent.

    _____

5. The man in the graveyard was <u>talking</u> to himself.

    _____

6. No one guessed that the woman in the <u>nice</u> clothes was a runaway slave.

    _____

Harriet Tubman was a slave, she didnt want to go to the South. But some mens were coming to take her to the south. She and her brother's runned away into the forest. I think they should just say they wont go to the south. The noises scared her brothers, they probably thought there was lots of big, feerce animals in that forest. But really only owls and frogs. They said their going back home. Harriet wanted to keep going, they wouldn't let her. Finully, she goes back to.

Unit 6
Notes to the Teacher

The following materials are to be used with *Is It Real?* (page 638) in *Scott Foresman Reading*.

Improve the Writing Sample (Use transparency 6 and the blackline masters on pages 154, 156.)
Show students the transparency, which gives a model of a 2-point writing sample based on the reading selection. You may also wish to photocopy the blackline version of the transparency so students have their own copy. Help students use the Writer's Checklist to evaluate the model and to make corrections and improvements. Write corrections on the transparency. Use the Guide for Writing Transparency 6 on page 152.

Answers to the exercise on page 154
1. The food on page 75 looks nasty and fake.
2. I would like to eat everything except for that round coconut thing.
3. The cupcake looked good with the chocolate frosting.

Improve Content (Use the blackline master on page 155.)
Students use elaboration to improve content. Once students have finished this exercise, you may want them to write their own response to the writing prompt on page 153. Remind them to use their graphic organizer and checklist. An example of a 6-point model appears on page 150.

Answers to the exercise on page 155
1. People often see art in grand old art museums.
2. The artwork *Black Gloves* appears to be a real pair of gloves.
3. Roman artists made floor mosaics that looked like unswept floors.
4. The painting *Fresh Roasted* shows a bin that holds roasted nuts.
5. *Traveler* is a sculpture of an exhausted tourist.

Writing Models and Evaluations

Writing Prompt Choose a picture from *Is It Real*? and another picture in this reading book. Compare and contrast the two pictures. Think about colors, shapes, how realistic the pictures are, and how each picture makes you feel. Which picture do you like better?

You might have students write in response to this prompt.

6-Point Score

The picture on page 75 looks like a breakfast table set with food like muffins, sausage, pancakes, and coffee. There are lots of round shapes. Like the bowls, plates, cups, and pancakes. Everythings a pretty boring color like brown or yellow or tan. This doesn't make it look too tasty, except for the muffins. The table looks like it's waiting for people. Some food in the bowls, maybe oatmeal and eggs, looks like it's been there for days. I wouldn't want to eat this food. It looks all stiff and cold.

I'd really like to eat the treats in *Strawberry Tart Supreme* though. Shapes are round like in the other picture. The colors in this picture are more brighter and shinier then in the breakfast picture. This picture shows desserts, which are my favorite things to eat. Desserts are much more interesting than breakfast anyway. I can just taste the chocolate frosting on that cupcake! That bright red strawberry tart with the whipped cream looks delicious. That swirly thing on the right looks good too. The food seems so gooey and real that it makes me drool. Now I'm hungry!

A 6 paper is OUTSTANDING. It demonstrates a high degree of proficiency in response to the assignment but may have a few minor errors.

An essay in this category:
- is well organized and coherently developed
- clearly explains or illustrates key ideas
- demonstrates syntactic variety
- clearly displays facility in the use of language
- is generally free from errors in mechanics, usage, and sentence structure

5-Point Score

I will compare contrast the picture on page 645 with the picture on page 594. The picture of *Strawberry Tart Supreme* looks very good. The strawberries look like they are dripping with juices and the whip cream looks tasty. The other treats look good to. The chocolate looks shiny and sweet and I'd love to take a bite. The problem with this painting is that it's a painting! It looks like a photograph. But its not.

The picture of the big brownie on page 594 looks good to. Even though I know its not real I can still think about what it would be like to eat it. The boy who is eating it looks happy. But the problem with this picture is that I know there are crushed up beetels in it! I can't even think about the crunch it would make. That's sick! It sure won't taste like how it looks. Both pictures look like something I'd like to eat at first but then I realize that niether would taste good for different reasons.

© Scott Foresman 5

A 5 paper is STRONG. It demonstrates clear proficiency in response to the assignment and may have minor errors.

An essay in this category:
- is generally well organized and coherently developed
- explains or illustrates key ideas
- demonstrates some syntactic variety
- displays facility in the use of language
- is generally free from errors in mechanics, usage, and sentence structure

4-Point Score

I am going to compare and contrast two dog pictures from my reading book. That dog on page 647 looks real, his paw comes right out at you! He looks like he might be pretty mean too. But he doesn't do anything. He just lays in that arch or whatever it is under the stares. I sure wouldn't want to have this dog for a pet.

The dog on page 59 doesn't look as real as the other one. I still like him better because he seems more friendlier. Like hes going to lick the girls face. He reminds me of the dog that we used to have. Rusty ran away last summer. The things were fuzzier in this picture, and theres more color and action. So if I had to choose, I'd go for the dog on page 59.

A 4 paper is COMPETENT. It demonstrates proficiency in response to the assignment.

An essay in this category:
- is adequately organized and developed
- explains or illustrates some of the key ideas
- displays adequate facility in the use of language
- may display some errors in mechanics, usage, or sentence structure

3-Point Score

There's a picture of a man on page 167 that looks a little like the man on page 641. They are both wearing blue shirts and have mustashes and they both have brown hair. Both on the ground. They even both have on sneakers. But one man is neeling and the other is sleeping. One man has a plane in the back and the other has bags. But the strangest of all is that the man on 167 is real and the other is fake! I'd never know. It looks like you could poke the man on 641 and he'd wake right up.

A 3 paper is LIMITED. It demonstrates some degree of proficiency in response to the assignment but is clearly flawed.

An essay in this category reveals one or more of the following weaknesses:
- inadequate organization or development
- inadequate explanation or illustration of key ideas
- limited or inappropriate word choice
- a pattern or accumulation of errors in mechanics, usage, or sentence structure

2-Point Score (See Writing Transparency 6.)

The food on page 75 looks nasty. And fake. I'll bet its been sitting their for an hour! The stuff in that picture on page 645 looks more good. Those strawberries look real. I would like to eat everything. Except for that round cokonut thing. I hate cokonut! The cupcake looked good. With the choclate frosting. You can bake this stuff for my freinds and I anytime.

Guide for Writing Transparency 6

A 2 paper is FLAWED. It demonstrates limited proficiency in response to the assignment.

An essay in this category reveals one or more of the following weaknesses:

- weak organization or very little development
- little or no relevant detail
- serious errors in mechanics, usage, sentence structure, or word choice

1-Point Score

The blak glove on page 640 are more nice then my ones they look like my dad glove. That baseball glove on page 101 look like my one what I lost las Yer. That is what I think of this glove.

A 1 paper is DEFICIENT. It demonstrates fundamental deficiencies in writing skills.

An essay in this category contains serious and persistent writing errors or is incoherent or is undeveloped.

0.0 is reported accompanied by one of the following codes to indicate a paper could not be scored for one of the following reasons:

A—Blank or Refusal
B—Illegible
C—Off Topic
D—Insufficient to Score
E—Predominantly in another language

Get Started

Literature Connection *Is It Real?* is a nonfictional article about art that tricks the viewer's eye. This selection begins on page 638 of your *Scott Foresman Reading* book. The author describes paintings and other art designed to fool the eye. This lesson also teaches about visualizing and comparing and contrasting things.

Visualizing, Comparing, and Contrasting You have learned that visualizing is creating a picture in your mind as you read. Comparing is telling how two or more things are alike. Contrasting is telling how two or more things are different.

Prepare to Write Read the prompt. Use the chart below to organize your ideas.

Writing Prompt Choose a picture from *Is It Real?* and another picture in this reading book. Compare and contrast the two pictures. Think about colors, shapes, how realistic the pictures are, and how each picture makes you feel. Which picture do you like better?

Title or Brief Description of Each Picture

_____ Page _____

_____ Page _____

Ways they are alike	Ways they are different
1. _____ _____ _____ 2. _____ _____ _____ 3. _____ _____ _____	1. _____ _____ _____ 2. _____ _____ _____ 3. _____ _____ _____

Improve the Writing Sample

Use a Writer's Checklist Your teacher will show you a writing transparency. Use the following writer's checklist to think of ways the writing could be improved.

Writer's Checklist

1. Look at the ideas.

___ Does the writer stick to the central idea, telling how a picture from *Is It Real?* and another picture are alike and different?

___ Are the similarities and differences clearly described?

___ Does the writer indicate which picture he or she likes better?

2. Look at the sentences.

___ Do all of the sentences express complete thoughts?

___ Do all of the sentences help explain similarities or differences between a picture from *Is It Real?* and another picture?

3. Look at the words.

___ Does the writer use words and details to help readers visualize the ways the pictures are alike and different?

4. Proofread to check for errors.

___ Does the writer use capital letters to begin sentences and proper nouns?

___ Does the writer use punctuation in each sentence?

___ Are the words spelled correctly?

Sentence Formation Combine the sentence with the sentence fragment that follows it. Remember to take out the first period and make the capital letter that follows it small. See the example below.

Example: You can bake this stuff. For my friends and me anytime.

_____You can bake this stuff for my friends and me anytime._____

1. The food on page 75 looks nasty. And fake.

_____

2. I would like to eat everything. Except for that round coconut thing.

_____

3. The cupcake looked good. With the chocolate frosting.

_____

Improve Content

Elaboration You can elaborate by adding or clarifying details and information. This will help your readers understand or visualize things more clearly.

Directions Improve each sentence by replacing the underlined word or phrase with a phrase that gives more information. Write your new sentence using a phrase from the box. See the example below.

Elaboration Box	
floor mosaics roasted nuts images that look real	pair of gloves an exhausted tourist grand old art museums

Example: Artists may try to trick viewers by painting <u>good pictures</u>.

    Artists may try to trick viewers by painting images that look real.

1. People often see art in <u>buildings</u>.

_____

2. The artwork *Black Gloves* appears to be a real <u>thing</u>.

_____

3. Roman artists made <u>surfaces</u> that looked like unswept floors.

_____

4. The painting *Fresh Roasted* shows a bin that holds <u>food</u>.

_____

5. *Traveler* is a sculpture of <u>a guy</u>.

_____

The food on page 75 looks nasty. And fake. I'll bet its been sitting their for an hour! The stuff in that picture on page 645 looks more good. Those strawberries look real. I would like to eat everything. Except for that round cokonut thing. I hate cokonut! The cupcake looked good. With the choclate frosting. You can bake this stuff for my freinds and I anytime.

Practice Tests

TerraNova Reading/ TCAP Writing

This section provides directions for administering two tests: a TerraNova Reading Practice Test and a TCAP Writing Practice Test. The purpose of these tests is to help students become familiar with the format and content of the Reading/Language Arts section of the TerraNova Test administered this year and the TCAP Writing Test given in the seventh grade. It will also help you assess a student's ability to meet the Tennessee English/Language Arts Curriculum Framework for Grades 3–5.

The TerraNova Reading Practice Test is a two-part test with seven passages and two types of multiple-choice questions: reading comprehension and language. The Writing Practice Test provides a writing prompt similar to the one given on the seventh-grade TCAP Writing Test.

The practice tests are not intended to be timed, but the information below will help you schedule testing sessions. You may want to administer each part of the TerraNova Reading Practice Test in a different session, or you may administer both parts in one testing session. Administer the TerraNova Practice Test shortly before you give the actual TerraNova Test. Give the TCAP Writing Practice Test toward the end of the year.

Test	Number of Questions	Estimated Time
Reading Part 1	30	45 min.
Reading Part 2	30	45 min.
Writing	1 Writing Prompt	50 min.

Directions for Administering the Tests

Give students and parents prior notice before administering a practice test. When you are ready to administer a practice test, make a copy of the test pages for each student. Tell students approximately how much time they have to complete the test. Describe the contents of the test and make sure students know where and how to mark their responses. Allow time for questions about directions before having students begin the test.

Write the starting time of the test on the board. For longer tests, you may wish to give short stretch breaks. Alert students when they have five minutes remaining before the end of the testing period.

Before administering the **TerraNova Reading Practice Test,** provide students with copies of the Student Answer Sheet on page 161. Have students write their names on their answer sheets. Read aloud the directions for correctly marking answers.

Then work through the samples on pages 162 to 163 as a class. Explain to students that the test they are about to take contains several similar passages with multiple-choice questions. Point out that each multiple-choice question has four answer choices: A, B, C, D or F, G, H, J. Students should choose the *best* answer to each question and mark the letter for the answer on the answer sheet.

Allow time for students to read the passage on page 162 and answer the sample questions. Then discuss the correct answers and how students knew these answers were the correct ones (Answers: 1. B; 2. H; 3. D). Walk around the room to make sure students have marked their answer sheets correctly. Let students know whether they are allowed to write in their test booklets. To assess and score students' tests, see the Answer Key on page 159.

A chart beginning on page 197 correlates each TerraNova Practice Test item to a learning expectation from the Tennessee English/Language Arts Curriculum Framework for Grades 3–5. This chart provides the Expectation, the number of the Practice Test item that covers the Expectation, and other assessment options.

Before administering the **TCAP Writing Practice Test,** provide students with scrap paper that they can use to plan and organize their writing. Also give them several copies of page 196 on which to write the final copy of their papers. Encourage students to use the checklist below the writing prompt to help them plan and check their papers. Make sure students understand that the final copy of their papers should be written on photocopies of page 196. Remind students to write their name at the top of each page of their final copies.

On page 160 is a 6-point scoring rubric. This is the same rubric used to score the seventh-grade TCAP Writing Test. Use it to evaluate student responses to the practice writing prompt. You may wish to duplicate this rubric for students and have them use it to evaluate and revise their own writing.

Answer Key

TerraNova Practice Test

Samples

S1. B
S2. H
S3. D

Part 1

1. A
2. F
3. D
4. F
5. D
6. H
7. B
8. H
9. D
10. F
11. C
12. J
13. B
14. F
15. D
16. H
17. A
18. H
19. D
20. G
21. D
22. H
23. C
24. F
25. D
26. F
27. D
28. G
29. B
30. G

Part 2

31. C
32. F
33. D
34. G
35. B
36. H
37. B
38. J
39. B
40. H
41. C
42. J
43. B
44. G
45. D
46. G
47. B
48. H
49. A
50. H
51. C
52. F
53. A
54. H
55. C
56. H
57. B
58. H
59. A
60. G

WRITING

6-Point Scoring Rubric for the Writing Prompt

6-Point Score

A 6 paper is OUTSTANDING. It demonstrates a high degree of proficiency in response to the assignment but may have a few minor errors.

An essay in this category:
- is well organized and coherently developed
- clearly explains or illustrates key ideas
- demonstrates syntactic variety
- clearly displays facility in the use of language
- is generally free from errors in mechanics, usage, and sentence structure

5-Point Score

A 5 paper is STRONG. It demonstrates clear proficiency in response to the assignment and may have minor errors.

An essay in this category:
- is generally well organized and coherently developed
- explains or illustrates key ideas
- demonstrates some syntactic variety
- displays facility in the use of language
- is generally free from errors in mechanics, usage, and sentence structure

4-Point Score

A 4 paper is COMPETENT. It demonstrates proficiency in response to the assignment.

An essay in this category:
- is adequately organized and developed
- explains or illustrates some of the key ideas
- demonstrates adequate facility in the use of language
- may display some errors in mechanics, usage, or sentence structure

3-Point Score

A 3 paper is LIMITED. It demonstrates some degree of proficiency in response to the assignment but is clearly flawed.

An essay in this category reveals one or more of the following weaknesses:
- inadequate organization or development
- inadequate explanation or illustration of key ideas
- limited or inappropriate word choice
- a pattern or accumulation of errors in mechanics, usage, or sentence structure

2-Point Score

A 2 paper is FLAWED. It demonstrates limited proficiency in response to the assignment.

An essay in this category reveals one or more of the following weaknesses:
- weak organization or very little development
- little or no relevant detail
- serious errors in mechanics, usage, sentence structure, or word choice

1-Point Score

A 1 paper is DEFICIENT. It demonstrates fundamental deficiencies in writing skills. An essay in this category contains serious and persistent writing errors or is incoherent or is undeveloped.

0.0 is reported accompanied by one of the following codes to indicate a paper could not be scored for one of the following reasons:
A—Blank or Refusal
B—Illegible
C—Off Topic
D—Insufficient to Score
E—Predominantly in another language

Student Answer Sheet

Student Name _____ Grade _____

Teacher Name _____ Date _____

Important Directions for Marking Answers

- Use black lead pencil (No. 2).
- Make heavy dark marks that fill the circle completely.
- Erase completely any answers you wish to change.
- If you erase a grid circle, do not redraw it.
- Do not make any stray marks on this answer sheet.

CORRECT MARK
Ⓐ ● Ⓒ Ⓓ

INCORRECT MARKS

SAMPLES
S1. Ⓐ Ⓑ Ⓒ Ⓓ
S2. Ⓕ Ⓖ Ⓗ Ⓙ
S3. Ⓐ Ⓑ Ⓒ Ⓓ

Part 1

1. Ⓐ Ⓑ Ⓒ Ⓓ	7. Ⓐ Ⓑ Ⓒ Ⓓ	13. Ⓐ Ⓑ Ⓒ Ⓓ	19. Ⓐ Ⓑ Ⓒ Ⓓ	25. Ⓐ Ⓑ Ⓒ Ⓓ
2. Ⓕ Ⓖ Ⓗ Ⓙ	8. Ⓕ Ⓖ Ⓗ Ⓙ	14. Ⓕ Ⓖ Ⓗ Ⓙ	20. Ⓕ Ⓖ Ⓗ Ⓙ	26. Ⓕ Ⓖ Ⓗ Ⓙ
3. Ⓐ Ⓑ Ⓒ Ⓓ	9. Ⓐ Ⓑ Ⓒ Ⓓ	15. Ⓐ Ⓑ Ⓒ Ⓓ	21. Ⓐ Ⓑ Ⓒ Ⓓ	27. Ⓐ Ⓑ Ⓒ Ⓓ
4. Ⓕ Ⓖ Ⓗ Ⓙ	10. Ⓕ Ⓖ Ⓗ Ⓙ	16. Ⓕ Ⓖ Ⓗ Ⓙ	22. Ⓕ Ⓖ Ⓗ Ⓙ	28. Ⓕ Ⓖ Ⓗ Ⓙ
5. Ⓐ Ⓑ Ⓒ Ⓓ	11. Ⓐ Ⓑ Ⓒ Ⓓ	17. Ⓐ Ⓑ Ⓒ Ⓓ	23. Ⓐ Ⓑ Ⓒ Ⓓ	29. Ⓐ Ⓑ Ⓒ Ⓓ
6. Ⓕ Ⓖ Ⓗ Ⓙ	12. Ⓕ Ⓖ Ⓗ Ⓙ	18. Ⓕ Ⓖ Ⓗ Ⓙ	24. Ⓕ Ⓖ Ⓗ Ⓙ	30. Ⓕ Ⓖ Ⓗ Ⓙ

Part 2

31. Ⓐ Ⓑ Ⓒ Ⓓ	37. Ⓐ Ⓑ Ⓒ Ⓓ	43. Ⓐ Ⓑ Ⓒ Ⓓ	49. Ⓐ Ⓑ Ⓒ Ⓓ	55. Ⓐ Ⓑ Ⓒ Ⓓ
32. Ⓕ Ⓖ Ⓗ Ⓙ	38. Ⓕ Ⓖ Ⓗ Ⓙ	44. Ⓕ Ⓖ Ⓗ Ⓙ	50. Ⓕ Ⓖ Ⓗ Ⓙ	56. Ⓕ Ⓖ Ⓗ Ⓙ
33. Ⓐ Ⓑ Ⓒ Ⓓ	39. Ⓐ Ⓑ Ⓒ Ⓓ	45. Ⓐ Ⓑ Ⓒ Ⓓ	51. Ⓐ Ⓑ Ⓒ Ⓓ	57. Ⓐ Ⓑ Ⓒ Ⓓ
34. Ⓕ Ⓖ Ⓗ Ⓙ	40. Ⓕ Ⓖ Ⓗ Ⓙ	46. Ⓕ Ⓖ Ⓗ Ⓙ	52. Ⓕ Ⓖ Ⓗ Ⓙ	58. Ⓕ Ⓖ Ⓗ Ⓙ
35. Ⓐ Ⓑ Ⓒ Ⓓ	41. Ⓐ Ⓑ Ⓒ Ⓓ	47. Ⓐ Ⓑ Ⓒ Ⓓ	53. Ⓐ Ⓑ Ⓒ Ⓓ	59. Ⓐ Ⓑ Ⓒ Ⓓ
36. Ⓕ Ⓖ Ⓗ Ⓙ	42. Ⓕ Ⓖ Ⓗ Ⓙ	48. Ⓕ Ⓖ Ⓗ Ⓙ	54. Ⓕ Ⓖ Ⓗ Ⓙ	60. Ⓕ Ⓖ Ⓗ Ⓙ

Reading and Language Arts

Sample Passage

Where's Dolly?

One evening at the Smithville Pet Center, a man ran in the door and grabbed Dolly. Before David could do anything, the man was gone. David called the police and then went back to cleaning cages.

For five days the store was very quiet. No one knew where the rare cockatoo could be. David worried that she might not be eating because birds like things to stay the same.

One Sunday night, Officer Hunt heard some loud talking at the end of a hall in a large apartment building. When he walked over to investigate, he found Dolly. She was talking to herself. She seemed to be fine, and he returned her to the pet store.

Sample A

S1 **This passage is mostly about**

   A   the eating habits of rare cockatoos

   B   the theft of a rare cockatoo

   C   David's job at a pet store

   D   how to teach cockatoos to talk

Sample B

A student wrote a paragraph about cockatoos. There are some mistakes that need correcting.

> [1] Cockatoos is a kind of parrot. [2] Most cockatoos are white, but some are pink, gray, or black. [3] Cockatoos are found in Australia, the East Indies, and the Philippines. [4] Cockatoos are intelligent and friendly birds they make good pets. [5] They sometimes can be trained to imitate human speech.

S2   **What is the best way to write Sentence 1?**

F   Cockatoos have been a kind of parrot.

G   Cockatoos were a kind of parrot.

H   Cockatoos are a kind of parrot.

J   Best as it is

S3   **Which sentence includes two separate thoughts that should be written as two sentences?**

A   Sentence 1

B   Sentence 2

C   Sentence 3

D   Sentence 4

Part 1

Communities

A community is a group of people living together, working together, or sharing common interests. This country is filled with many different kinds of communities. Every community is unique. This theme will take a look inside various communities. You will read about community celebrations and activities, and you will explore how people work together to make communities better for everyone.

Directions

In this story, you will read about a special birthday celebration. You may have heard of a "Sweet Sixteen" party. However, in Carly Garcia's Mexican-American community, *fifteen* is the most special birthday year of all. Read the story to learn about *Quinceañera*. Then answer Numbers 1 through 6.

Growing-Up Celebrations

by Melissa Mendez

Carly Garcia woke up with a feeling of anticipation. It was Saturday morning, and she had a big day ahead of her. She was expecting a great day because it was her sister Maria's fifteenth birthday. In Carly's family, a girl's fifteenth birthday is special because it is a Quinceañera (keen-say-ahn-yay-rah).

Quinceañera is a tradition that started in ancient Mexico. According to tradition, the fifteenth birthday celebrates the beginning of a journey into adulthood. The word *quinceañera* comes from the Spanish words *quince* (keen-say) for "fifteen," and *años* (ahn-yos), which means "years."

Carly had helped her sister and parents plan the celebration. She felt like she was part of something very important. The party was to take place at the Garcia's house. Carly had already decorated most of the house and yard with flowers, streamers, and balloons the night before, but there was a bit of work left to do.

GO ON

They had even set up a party tent in the backyard. Food was going to be a big part of the celebration. Carly and her parents had prepared a large buffet of tamales, chicharrones, carnitas, tortillas, and salsa. They would keep the table filled with delicious treats, so their guests could help themselves all night long.

The cake was also an important part of the celebration. Carly's aunt had brought it over the night before. It is a tradition that the girl turning fifteen cuts the first piece of cake. Maria would not see it until the party began. Carly, however, had taken a peek at the cake. It was beautifully decorated with frosting flowers. Across the middle was written *Felicidades* (fay-lee-see-dah-days), which means "Congratulations." On top of the cake was a little statue of a fifteen-year-old girl. Carly knew that Maria would save it.

Maria then would receive a special present from one of her aunts. It would be a doll, to represent her last gift as a child. The doll had a skirt made up of individual bows that each had Maria's name and her birth date written on them. This doll would be placed on the main table. Each guest would take one of the bows at the end of the evening.

Carly was looking forward to the dancing most of all. Her cousin's band was going to set up on their back deck. They would play all different kinds of music so that everyone from young to old would enjoy dancing. The first dance would be for Maria and her father. Carly couldn't wait until the day when the first dance would belong to her.

1   *Quinceañera* **is a tradition from which country?**

A   Mexico

B   Argentina

C   Spain

D   Cuba

2   **According to the passage, why is a girl's fifteenth birthday special?**

F   It marks the beginning of adulthood.

G   It means a girl can now go to big parties.

H   It is the first time a girl dances in public with her father.

J   It means a girl can no longer buy dolls.

3 In this story, "Carly and her parents had prepared a large buffet of tamales, chicharrones, carnitas, tortillas, and salsa." What happens at a buffet dinner?

A You go to a fancy restaurant where you are served by waiters.

B You go to the drive-through window at a take-out restaurant.

C All the guests sit down at a table and are served.

D Guests serve themselves from a table of food and drinks.

4 Which idea helps you know that your answer to Number 3 is right?

F The guests help themselves all night.

G The food is traditional Mexican food.

H This is an important event.

J There is a cake and dancing.

5 Why do you think Maria would not see the cake until the party began?

A It was supposed to be a surprise.

B Maria did not want to see anything in advance.

C Maria didn't know there was going to be a cake.

D It is a tradition that is part of *Quinceañera*.

6 The story says, "Carly Garcia woke up with a feeling of anticipation." The word *anticipation* probably means the same as

F tiredness

G sadness

H eagerness

J happiness

Directions

After she read "Growing-Up Celebrations," Dixie wrote her own story about a celebration in her community. Here is Dixie's story. There are several mistakes that need correcting.

> [1] Every year, my town having a huge celebration for the Fourth of July. [2] First we all go to the cookout at Town Hall. [3] At the cookout, we have the best barbecued food in the world. [4] We also have games, rides, and a prize raffle. [5] Then we have a dance the deejay from the best radio station plays songs until we are all too tired to stand. [6] Last we all settle down for the fireworks. [7] I've seen lots of fireworks on TV, but none are as amazing as ours.

7 **Choose the best way to write Sentence 1.**

A   Every year, my town have a huge celebration for the Fourth of July.

B   Every year, my town has a huge celebration for the Fourth of July.

C   Every year, my town was having a huge celebration for the Fourth of July.

D   Best as it is

8 **Which sentence contains two complete thoughts and should be written as two sentences?**

F   Sentence 3

G   Sentence 4

H   Sentence 5

J   Sentence 6

9 **Where would this sentence best fit in the paragraph?**

Last year, I even won a new computer!

A   after Sentence 1

B   after Sentence 2

C   after Sentence 3

D   after Sentence 4

© Scott Foresman 5

This is an article about a city where bikes are left unlocked for other people to use. Find out why it's a good idea for the city and even the planet! Read the story, and then answer Numbers 10 through 16.

Neighborhood Bikes

by Evelina Zarkh

Have you been to Austin, Texas, recently and noticed a new phenomenon? It's truly a strange sight. People are riding yellow bikes in the downtown and college areas and leaving them where they stop for another person to use.

The Yellow Bike Project started with two dozen bright yellow community bikes. They have been put into service as free transportation for commuters who live in the suburbs and work in central Austin. It discourages people from using their cars when they need to make short trips within the city.

The Yellow Bike Project is modeled after the Red Bike program in Madison, Wisconsin. Like the Red Bike program, the Austin program might be considered a cab service without the driver—or the fare! A person can ride a yellow bike anywhere, but after the rider reaches the destination the bike is to be placed unlocked in an open area. Like a cab, the bicycle may not wait around for its last rider.

People are encouraged to use them whenever they have to run errands or get somewhere nearby, instead of using a car. The yellow bikes are there to help people get daily errands done a little bit faster, and they're better for the environment. People can pick up a bike anywhere in central Austin, use it to get wherever they need to go, and just leave it when they've reached their destinations. It's important for everyone to leave the bikes in places where other riders can easily find them.

The program is free for anyone to use because the people who work on the Yellow Bike Project are volunteers, and the bikes are donations. The volunteers also run a shop for selling and repairing used bikes.

GO ON

The Goals of the Yellow Bike Project

 Recycle a wasted resource by recovering bikes that have been forgotten in the garage and other dead-end places.

 Give skills to youth by training them to repair bikes.

 Promote local businesses by locating bike stations at participating businesses and by providing a free and easy way for shoppers and sightseers to move about the city.

 Create a sense of community by offering a distinct and colorful form of transportation that helps people get to know their neighborhoods and cities in a way that automobiles don't allow.

 Promote cleaner air by using one of the most efficient machines ever invented. Bikes provide a healthy and enjoyable alternative to automobiles. They don't pollute the air, and they offer great exercise!

10 **What city has the Yellow Bike Project?**

F Austin

G Madison

H Dallas

J Chicago

11 **Which statement best describes the purpose of the Yellow Bike Project?**

A Its purpose is to put local cab companies out of business.

B It is a way to attract tourists to the city.

C It promotes cleaner air and a sense of community.

D It's a plan to make some people rich.

12 The passage says that the Yellow Bike Project provides free transportation for commuters who live in the suburbs and work in central Austin. *Commuters* are people who

   F   have important jobs

   G   shop often in the city

   H   live in the suburbs

   J   live in one place and travel to another for work

13 What is the most likely reason why the bikes are all painted yellow?

   A   It helps drivers see the bikes on the road.

   B   It lets people know the bikes are part of the Yellow Bike Project.

   C   Someone in the Yellow Bike Project likes the color yellow.

   D   The program was recycling leftover yellow paint.

14 How does the Yellow Bike Project work like a cab service?

   F   It helps people get around the city.

   G   It gets people out to the country.

   H   It makes money for some people.

   J   It promotes clean air.

15 Which of the following is <u>not</u> true of the Yellow Bike Project?

   A   Anyone can use the yellow bikes.

   B   Yellow bikes do not pollute the air.

   C   You don't have to pay to use the yellow bikes.

   D   People earn money when they sell a bike to the program.

16 **Which of the following sentences best combines these two sentences into one?**

The Yellow Bike Project helps people get around.

The project also helps the environment.

- **F** The Yellow Bike Project helps people get around and the project also helps the environment.
- **G** The Yellow Bike Project helps people get around, although it helps the environment.
- **H** The Yellow Bike Project helps people get around and also helps the environment.
- **J** The Yellow Bike Project helps people get around the environment.

Directions

For Numbers 17 and 18, choose the sentence that is complete and written correctly.

17
- **A** Riding a bike is a great way to exercise.
- **B** Bikes don't causing any pollution problems.
- **C** Cars may be a problem their fumes can hurt the air.
- **D** The air that is polluted with exhaust.

18
- **F** When people get together to make a difference.
- **G** The yellow bikes community spirit.
- **H** We should all do more to make our cities cleaner.
- **J** Riding a bike for free and leaving it anywhere.

Directions

Senegal is a country in Africa. Read this passage to learn more about Ibrahima, a young man who has left his African home to begin a new life in New York City. Then answer Numbers 19 through 23.

Learning American Business: A Young Man in New York

by Victoria Ebin

Every morning, Ibrahima carries two well-worn bags filled with African beaded bracelets, baseball caps, and school bags to 14th Street in New York City. On the corner of 6th Avenue, he sets up a table in front of a clothing store and carefully lays out his merchandise. Sometimes business is good, but on rainy days, Ibrahima makes few sales and passes the day talking with the other Senegalese street vendors.

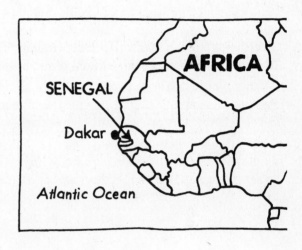

Ibrahima is only 18. He left his village in western Senegal last year to join his Uncle Dramane in New York. Uncle Dramane sent the money for Ibrahima's airplane ticket, and now Ibrahima will repay him by helping with his business.

Ibrahima's family used to be well-off. They had many farms and grew peanuts. But for several years, there has been no rain, and the countryside where they live has become a windy dust bowl. The drought and lack of jobs in the towns have forced many thousands of Senegalese to leave their homes and families to look for work in other countries, especially Europe and the United States. Tens of thousands of young Senegalese vendors now work the streets of France, Italy, Germany, Spain, and the United States.

These young men generally start out like Ibrahima, selling small items. As they become successful, they use their savings to buy more expensive merchandise, such as cameras, radios, and stereos, which they send back to Senegal by boat. Because they keep in close touch with their families at home, they can call an uncle or a brother who is a trader and tell him to pick up their merchandise when it arrives at the port of Dakar. The relative will then resell the merchandise at a very large profit.

GO ON

One reason Senegalese traders have become so successful is that most of them belong to a religious organization called the Mouride brotherhood. (Mouride is an Arabic word meaning "disciple.") The Mourides help each other; they work together and say they trust each other.

The Mourides are Muslim, like 90 percent of the population of Senegal. The brotherhood has its own saint, named Cheikh Amadu Bamba, who has been dead for more than 50 years. He is worshipped as the religious leader and protector of his followers.

Many of the traders in New York belong to the Mouride brotherhood. The Mourides also control trade in Senegal. They run the big markets in Dakar, where you can buy everything from dried fish to shoes and computers. In Dakar's Sandaga market, the largest market in the country, more than 75 percent of the traders are Mourides.

Ibrahima's Uncle Dramane, for example, who became rich by selling cloth in Sandaga market, says that he succeeded only because he is a Mouride. When he traveled to the Middle East and Europe to buy the most beautiful cloth he could find for Senegalese women to make their long robes (*boubous*), he said that he knew he could count on Mouride brothers for a place to stay. Other Mourides back in Dakar sold the cloth for him and handed over the money when he returned.

Dramane later went to New York, and now he specializes in buying televisions, which he sends back to his cousin, another Mouride, who has an electronics store in Dakar. He is now training Ibrahima to help him so that if he must travel, Ibrahima can take care of the business.

Ibrahima is learning to buy and sell and to bargain with customers. He says that he is an apprentice, just like his friends back in Senegal who learned to become carpenters or mechanics by working with skilled craftsmen.

Ibrahima dreams that one day he can return to Senegal with enough savings to start a chicken farm, but he knows that many people back in Senegal count on him to send money home so that they can eat. He says he will be patient.

19 **Where is Ibrahima originally from?**

A   New York City

B   France

C   Germany

D   Senegal

20 **Why did Ibrahima's family leave their farm?**

F   They wanted to get rich.

G   A change in the weather made farming difficult.

H   Senegal became unsafe for them.

J   They lost their farm to the bank.

21 **What did Ibrahima's Uncle Dramane mostly sell before he moved to New York?**

A   televisions

B   cameras

C   stereos

D   cloth

22 **What has helped Senegalese traders become so successful?**

F   They are smarter than other people.

G   They have more money to start with.

H   They cooperate with each other.

J   They operate all over the world.

23 **In which of these resources would you probably find a map of Senegal?**

A **B** **C** **D**

GO ON

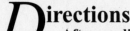

After reading about Ibrahima and the Senegalese traders, one class decided to have a street fair to raise money. Tommy made the poster below. There are a couple of mistakes that need correcting.

Make sure you are on Number 24 on your answer sheet.

It's the
Fifth-Grade Street Fair
at Hunnewell Elementary School

Saturday, June 5
10:00 a.m.–5:00 p.m.
Parking Lot

¹ Come and spend the day playing games and browsing the booths.

² Admire or purchase the beautiful artwork of the fifth-grade class. We have paintings, pottery, and handmade jewelry.

³ Enter to win electronic equipment donated from the Electronics Super Store.

⁴ All profits will go to the fifth-grade class trip fund.

⁵ We hope you will joining us for the fun.

---

24 **What is the best way to write Sentence 5?**

F We hope you will join us for the fun!

G We hoped you will joining us for the fun?

H We hoping you will join us for the fun.

J Best as it is

25 **Which sentence would best follow Sentence 4?**

A Maybe you will win the new flat TV!

B All the pottery is donated by local potter, Mr. Bixby.

C We'll have ring tosses, three-legged races, and a dunk tank.

D We hope to raise enough money to go to New York City.

26 Which set of notes captures the most important information from Tommy's poster?

Fifth-Grade Street Fair
June 5
10:00 a.m.–5:00 p.m.
Parking Lot

F

Fifth-Grade Steet Fair
Electronics Super Store
Saturday
Parking Lot

G

Parking Lot
Electronics Super Store
June 5
10:00 a.m.–5:00 p.m.

H

Saturday
10:00 a.m.–5:00 p.m.
Parking Lot
June 5

J

GO ON

Directions

Now you will read about a club that has a lot to offer kids and the community. It provides many opportunities for young people to learn about everything from goats to the Internet. Read the passage. Then answer Numbers 27 through 30.

Head, Heart, Hands, and Health

by Lori Andres

Do you know of an organization for young people that has something for everyone, costs nothing to join, and is actually fun? A program called 4-H is all of these things!

4-H started around 1900 with the main goal of teaching young people about agriculture, or the science of farming. It was also started as an effort to help young people become good citizens. The abbreviation 4-H stands for the program's pledge that says, "*For* my club, my community, my country and my world, I pledge my *head* to clearer thinking, my *heart* to greater loyalty, my *hands* to larger service, and my *health* to better living." This pledge truly summarizes the goals of 4-H.

Today, 4-H is about much more than farming. 4-H has camps where participants learn about leadership, teamwork, and self-confidence. 4-H is also a program that believes in teaching kids a variety of useful skills. Programs teach young people how to catch fish, use computers, fix bikes, and even create websites.

4-H clubs also take part in volunteering. Across the U.S., 4-H kids are cleaning up trash in their communities, helping in literacy projects, and delivering food to people in need.

Agriculture, however, remains an important part of 4-H. For example, there are programs in horsemanship and in raising livestock such as cattle, pigs, and sheep. 4-H groups in different areas have their own specific projects.

For example, one 4-H club raises goats. The kids learn how to keep the goats healthy. They learn to trim the goats' hooves and to milk the dairy goats. The club members take the best-looking goats to compete at goat shows and agricultural fairs. They also bring the gentlest goats to petting zoos. Some of the kids in the program learn about computers too and have created a website about raising goats.

4-H has many programs pertaining to other animals as well. In some places kids learn how to train a dog, how to take care of a cat, or how to breed hamsters. If you think you might want to be a veterinarian, 4-H offers a veterinary science program. Whatever it is you're looking for, chances are that 4-H can help you find it!

27 **What do members of the 4-H Club pledge their hearts to?**

A   clearer thinking   **C**   larger service

B   better living   **D**   greater loyalty

28 **Which of the following is the best way to describe 4-H?**

F   4-H is a club that focuses only on agriculture and veterinary science.

G   4-H offers many activities and helps children develop strong character.

H   4-H participants raise goats and bring them to agricultural fairs.

J   4-H has not changed since it was founded in 1900.

29 **Why do members select the gentlest goats to take to the petting zoo?**

A   These goats are smaller than other goats.

B   These goats are less likely to bite someone when petted.

C   These goats are the best-looking goats.

D   These goats can also be milked.

30 **Which sentences best support this topic sentence?**

Members of the local 4-H club were excited about the upcoming agricultural fair.

F   4-H clubs offer many different activities for kids. Some clubs even have hamster breeding and veterinary science programs.

G   The group had been busy all week washing and grooming their goats. They were sure they would take the blue ribbon in at least one event.

H   The group had been working on their website all month. The kids were especially proud of their graphics and exciting links.

J   They were learning to become good citizens. They also had gained self-confidence.

Part 2

Address:
Earth

Earth is an amazing and fascinating place. From destructive tornadoes to beautiful rain forests, there are frightening and wonderful things happening and growing on our planet. In this section you will read about earthquakes and tornadoes. You will also learn how to take care of our precious home and limit pollution. So read on to find out more about our home, Earth.

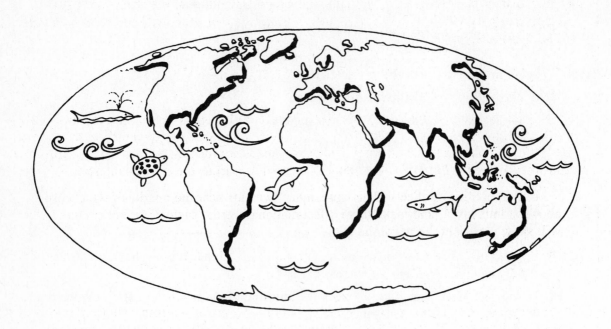

An Edible Earthquake

by Rebecca Schwartz

Have you ever wondered why earthquakes occur along fault lines? Earth's crust sometimes gets pulled apart by outside forces. This creates small breaks, called tension fractures. These fractures can join together to form larger fault lines. Usually, the larger the fault line, the more the ground will move and break apart during an earthquake. Here's an experiment that demonstrates how this happens. Best of all, it's an edible experiment. You can eat it when you're finished!

Materials: A few pieces of pre-sliced American cheese (the thin slices that are individually wrapped in plastic work best)

Steps:

1. Unwrap a slice of cheese. Hold it by the edges. Now pull. The cheese should tear apart. Do the same thing with another slice of cheese. It will also tear apart, but if you compare the two slices, they probably did not tear in the same place.

2. Take another slice of cheese. Make a small cut in the middle of the cheese with your fingernail or a butter knife. This cut should be parallel, or even, with the edges you will pull. Now pull on the two edges.

Even though the cut you made was small, it created a fault in the cheese. Because this fault weakens the cheese, it usually is the first place to tear when you pull on the cheese. If you make a cut in the same place on another slice of cheese, it probably will tear in the same place. Do you notice that the cheese gets easier to pull apart as the cut gets bigger?

3. Take another slice of cheese. This time, make two cuts near the middle of the cheese, about an inch apart, and make them offset diagonally from each other. The picture below will show you where to make the cuts.

This time, when you pull on the edges, the tears probably will start from each fault line. As the tears get bigger, they will curve toward each other and finally become one large tear. Again, as the tears gets bigger, the cheese will pull apart faster and more easily.

You have created tension fractures and fault lines with cheese. This should help you understand how the earth's crust pulls apart during an earthquake. Now you can eat the cheese!

GO ON

© Scott Foresman 5

31 **Which statement best summarizes the purpose of the experiment?**

A to play with American cheese

B to learn about earthquakes

C to show how tension fractures can lead to earthquakes

D to practice making tension fractures in the cheese

32 **What is the first step in the experiment?**

F Unwrap a slice of American cheese.

G Eat the cheese.

H Make a small slice in the cheese.

J Pull the cheese apart.

33 **What do the cuts in the cheese represent?**

A mountains

B outside forces that pull on Earth's crust

C humans

D tension fractures

34 **Which of the following is a true statement?**

F The cheese will not tear near a parallel cut.

G The two small cuts in the cheese will turn into one large tear.

H The cuts do not need to be parallel to the edges of the slice of cheese.

J The cheese gets harder to pull apart as the cuts get bigger.

35 **The passage says, ". . . earthquakes occur along fault lines." What is a *fault line*?**

A a small break in Earth's crust

B a large break in Earth's crust

C a parallel line

D another name for an earthquake

36 **Which word best fits both sentences?**

It was not Jack's _____ that he missed the bus.

Many earthquakes happen along _____ lines.

F problem

G tension

H fault

J fracture

© Scott Foresman 5

Directions

Students in Mr. Smith's class are working on reports about earthquakes.
Here are some questions related to their work.

37 Which of the sentences below best combines these two sentences into one?

Mr. Smith's class made a model of an earthquake.

The model trembled and shook like an earthquake.

A Mr. Smith's class made a model of an earthquake, but the model trembled and shook like the real earthquake.

B Mr. Smith's class made a model earthquake that trembled and shook like an earthquake.

C Making a model of an earthquake, Mr. Smith's class trembled and shook like an earthquake.

D Mr. Smith's class made a model of an earthquake though the model was trembling and shaking.

38 In which of these resources would Tyrone find out more about what causes an earthquake?

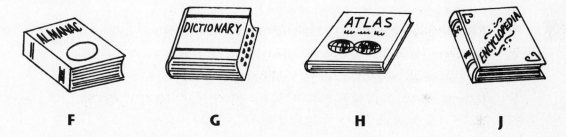

F　　　　　　**G**　　　　　　**H**　　　　　　**J**

39 Suzanne was reading an article about earthquakes. Under which heading would she probably find information about the San Andreas Fault in California?

A The World's Most Destructive Earthquakes

B Famous Fault Lines

C The Richter Scale

D A Timeline of Japanese Earthquakes

Here is a report that Mr. Smith's class wrote. It has some mistakes that need correcting.

¹ An earthquake cause by vibrations in the earth's crust. ² Sometimes forces pushing on a mass of rock overpower the friction holding it in place. ³ This makes blocks of rock slip against each other. ⁴ The slippage makes shock waves that travel through the earth. ⁵ The shock waves are recorded at research stations. ⁶ There have been some terrible earthquakes in California. ⁷ Then scientists called seismologists rank the earthquake on a scale of 1 to 9 this is called the Richter scale.

40 **What is the best way to write Sentence 1?**

F An earthquake is causing by vibrations in the earth's crust.

G An earthquake will cause from vibrations in the earth's crust.

H An earthquake is caused by vibrations in the earth's crust.

J Best as it is

41 **Which sentence does not belong in this paragraph?**

A Sentence 4

B Sentence 5

C Sentence 6

D Sentence 7

42 **Which sentence includes two separate thoughts that should be written as two sentences?**

F Sentence 4

G Sentence 5

H Sentence 6

J Sentence 7

© Scott Foresman 5

Directions

The following article includes many facts about the power of tornadoes and what to do when one occurs. Read the article. The answer Numbers 43 through 50.

Tornado Power

by Michael Sandler

Normally we think of wind as a helpful thing. A cool breeze refreshes us on a hot day. A good stiff wind can move a sailboat. We even use windmills to convert the wind's energy to electricity. But when winds go over 40 miles an hour, they can cause damage. Inside a hurricane, winds may blow at over 75 miles an hour. Inside a tornado, winds range from 40 miles an hour up to 320 miles an hour.

In the United States, about one percent of our thunderstorms produce tornadoes. Thunderstorms start when warm, moist air meets cold, dry air. In a tornado, the warm air pushes up through the layer of cold air. The warm air starts to rotate and spin upwards in a spiral. Tornadoes are rated on a scale from F0 to F5. As you see in the chart on the next page, about 74 percent of tornadoes in the U.S. are rated as weak (F0 or F1).

There is tremendous power inside tornadoes and thunderstorms. The average thunderstorm releases about ten million kilowatt-hours of energy. That's enough electrical energy to power a thousand homes for at least a year. So far, we have no way to use that energy. Imagine what we could do if we could find a way to harness all that energy!

When the weather looks like there might be tornadoes soon, the National Weather Service issues a tornado watch. This gives people a chance to get the family together and get ready to go to the safest place in their home if necessary. When a tornado warning is issued, it means a tornado has been spotted. This is the time to go to the safest place in the house immediately.

If you live in an area that often experiences tornadoes, it's a good idea to make tornado warning plans with your family. Make sure that everyone knows where to go and what to do, so everyone stays safe.

The Fujita-Pearson Tornado Intensity Scale				
F-Scale Number	Intensity Phrase	Wind speed mph (miles per hour)	Rating	Approximate percentage in U.S.
F0	Gale	40–72 mph	Weak	} 74%
F1	Moderate	73–112 mph	Weak	
F2	Significant	113–157 mph	Strong	} 25%
F3	Severe	158–206 mph	Strong	
F4	Devastating	207–260 mph	Violent	} 1%
F5	Incredible	261+ mph	Violent	

43 **This passage is mostly about**

   A how destructive tornadoes can be

   B what tornadoes are and how to react to one

   C how an F1 tornado differs from other tornadoes

   D why you shouldn't worry about tornadoes

44 **Winds do not cause damage until they exceed speeds of**

   F 25 mph

   G 40 mph

   H 75 mph

   J 112 mph

45 **The movement of a *spiral* is most closely related to the movement of**

   A a tractor pulling a heavy load

   B a bicycle speeding down a hill

   C an ice cream truck stopped at the corner

   D a spinning top

46 **When a tornado has been spotted, the National Weather Service issues a**

   F tornado watch

   G tornado warning

   H tornado drill

   J tornado siren

© Scott Foresman 5

47   What would be the best thing to do if there is a bad thunderstorm in your area?

   A   Don't do anything because most thunderstorms don't turn into tornadoes.

   B   Stay inside and find out if a tornado watch or a warning has been issued.

   C   Go outside and look for tornadoes.

   D   Run immediately to the safest place in your house.

48   What percentage of tornadoes in the U.S. are rated strong or violent?

   F   24%

   G   25%

   H   26%

   J   74%

49   This article could be used to help answer which of the following questions?

   A   What causes a tornado to form?

   B   Where is the safest place to go if you see a tornado?

   C   Where are tornadoes most likely to happen?

   D   What are some famous tornadoes that have caused severe damage?

50   Choose the sentence that is complete and written correctly.

   F   A tornado are a very powerful storm.

   G   It have incredibly strong winds.

   H   It can be very dangerous.

   J   If you spot a tornado, to the basement.

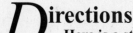

Directions

Here is a story one student wrote about his experience with a bad storm. For Numbers 51 and 52, choose the sentences that best complete the paragraph.

> Last spring, I had a frightening experience. It had been hot and humid all day. By late afternoon, a terrible thunderstorm had arrived. _____**(51)**_____ The sky turned yellow, and the wind began to blow all the leaves off the trees. I had never seen anything like it. I started to feel nervous. _____**(52)**_____

51 **A** Recently a tornado passed through our town.

      B That morning, I went for a swim.

      C Soon I knew it wasn't an ordinary thunderstorm.

      D After it was over, we saw many damaged homes and trees.

52 **F** That's when my whole family went down to the basement.

      G I went outside to get a better look.

      H I love thunderstorms because they're fun.

      J It was just another boring night in my town.

Directions
What can you do to help the earth? Read the selection below and find out
what others have done and how you can pitch in. Then answer Numbers 53
through 58.

How to Help Save Our Home Planet

by George Laycock

A long time ago after lightning started a fire, some curious person carried a burning stick back to his cave. He became the first man to use fire. Soon people were using fire to keep warm, cook meat, and scare tigers away.

This was just the beginning. After thousands of years, in addition to wood, we learned to burn coal, oil, and natural gas. Now we burn those fossil fuels all over the world to heat our homes and run automobiles, trucks, power plants, and factories.

That original fire maker probably created the world's first man-made air pollution. But that little bit of smoke was no big problem.

Today, however, there are five *billion* people helping pollute the world. And it's getting worse. The good news is that every one of us can do something to help solve the problem.

Around Home

For most of us the best opportunity to make a difference in the environment comes right in our own homes.

For starters, turn lights off when they are not needed. During the day, open the curtains and use natural light. At night, when you leave a room, flip off the light switch.

© Scott Foresman 5

From "How to Help Save Our Home Planet" by George Laycock from *Boys' Life* Magazine, May 1991, pp. 24, 25–27, & 55. Reprinted by permission of George Laycock.

GO ON

Use lower-wattage bulbs where you don't need much light for safety or reading.

Burning light bulbs warm the air. This means more electricity is needed to run the air conditioner.

Replace standard bulbs with the new compact fluorescent bulbs. They cost more but you get the same amount of light for about one-fourth the electricity. And they last five to 10 years.

In summer, set the air conditioner a few degrees higher to save energy. In winter, wear a sweater and set the heat a little lower.

Don't run the family washer, dryer, or dishwasher for just a few items. Wait until the machines are full.

Turn off the television when nobody is watching it.

Keep the refrigerator closed as much as possible.

Every time you save electricity you reduce pollution. About 65 percent of the sulfur dioxide that causes acid rain comes from the power plants that produce our electricity.

Save Water

We seldom think about water costing money, but it costs to purify it, pipe it to your house, and heat it.

Here are several ways you can save water:

Take a shower rather than a bath. A shower can use less water. Use a water-saving shower nozzle.

Do not let the water run while you're brushing your teeth. This alone can save five gallons of water each time you brush.

Repair dripping faucets.

If you have to water the lawn, do it in the cool early morning when less water evaporates.

Recycle

Find the nearest recycling center. Ask what materials they accept. Some pay cash for cans, paper, and glass. Separate the recyclable items from your trash and collect them in separate containers. Set aside a corner of the basement or garage for recycling.

Some cities now collect these items for recycling right at the curb in front of your home. Your city has no such program? Then encourage city leaders to start one.

Along with recycling, try to use less paper and other materials. Saving paper saves trees. Use the backs of old papers for practicing your homework. Don't throw away your junk mail; use the envelopes for notepaper.

Instead of reaching for a paper towel, keep a cloth towel handy.

Two California seventh graders, Andrea Clark and Emily Forster, wanted to help save tropical rain forests from the chain saws. They knew that rain forests help clean the earth's air of carbon dioxide and help control our climate. And half the world's species of animals live in these wet forests.

Andrea and Emily got their whole school to help, and collected and sold aluminum cans to buy and save 11 acres of rain forest at $50 an acre.

© Scott Foresman 5

One Boy's Success

If you think one young person can't make a difference, then meet Andrew Holleman of Chelmsford, MA. When Andrew was 12, he learned that a developer planned to build a housing project on 42 acres of nearby swampy woodland.

This woods happened to be one of Andrew's favorite places. He knew every foot of it. He went there to study the snakes, turtles, birds, and plants for his Scout projects. He thought it was too swampy to be a good place for houses.

He studied the laws about wetlands. Then he asked all the neighbors to sign his petition to stop the development.

Tests eventually showed that Andrew was right: The wet soil would not be a good place for the new community's sewage system.

He went to public meetings. The builder's lawyers spoke in favor of the new houses. Andrew also stood up and talked to the people. He quoted the law and explained why this woods should be saved for the future.

As a result, his favorite woods is still there. Andrew proved what young conservationists everywhere should know—their work for the environment can make a big difference.

53 **What happens when you leave a refrigerator door open for a period of time?**

A The refrigerator uses more energy to keep things cool.

B The refrigerator uses less energy to keep things cool.

C The refrigerator uses about the same amount of energy with the door open or closed.

D The light in the refrigerator will turn off.

54 **Why did Andrew Holleman work to stop a housing project from being built in his neighborhood?**

F He didn't want new people moving into his neighborhood.

G He was concerned that the builders would make a lot of noise and mess.

H He wanted to save his favorite woods from being cut down.

J He felt people should buy older homes, not new ones.

55 **Which of the following home chores will not help prevent pollution?**

A turning off lights when leaving the room

B turning off the television when not watching it

C cleaning your room

D running appliances only with full loads

56 **What advice do you think the author would give to someone who wanted to help save the planet?**

F There is no easy way to help save the planet.

G The problem of pollution is too big for any one person to try to solve.

H Each of us can do something to help save the planet.

J Stop using electricity and move out to the country.

57 **Why do you think the author described Andrew Holleman's efforts to stop the housing project?**

A He wanted readers to stop housing projects in their neighborhood.

B He wanted to show that one person can make a difference to the environment.

C He wanted to show how petitions are the best way to save the environment.

D He wanted to explain why swamps are not good places for sewage systems.

58 **The article calls Andrew Holleman a *conservationist* for saving his favorite woods. A *conservationist* is someone who**

F builds housing projects

G uses something as often as possible

H protects forest, rivers, and other natural resources from harm

J wants to keep things as they are or were in the past

Directions

Here is a paragraph a student wrote after reading about how he could help save the planet. It has some mistakes that need correcting.

> [1] I had never recycled anything before I read this article. [2] I didn't think it could possibly make a difference. [3] Now I realize that every effort to cut down on garbage counts. [4] I walk to school, too. [5] I have encouraged my family to join me in recycling by setting up a new garbage can for recycling only. [6] Recycling was more easier than I had imagined!

59 Choose the best way to write Sentence 6.

A Recycling was easier than I had imagined!

B Recycling was more easily than I had imagined!

C Recycling was easy than I had imagined!

D Best as it is

60 Which sentence does <u>not</u> belong in this paragraph?

F Sentence 3

G Sentence 4

H Sentence 5

J Sentence 6

TCAP Practice Writing Test

Write a paper about a special place. It might be a place you visited on vacation or a room or a treehouse that you enjoy. Tell what the place is, how you found it, and why it is special to you.

Writer's Checklist

1   Read over your paper.

_____ Did you focus on one main idea?

_____ Did you use enough details so that readers will understand what you describe?

_____ Is your paper written in a logical order?

_____ Will readers know how you feel about the special place you describe?

2   Think about the sentences and words you have used.

_____ Did you use sentences of different lengths?

_____ Did you use different kinds of sentences?

_____ Did you use vivid words to describe things, places, and people?

_____ Did you use verbs and pronouns correctly?

3   Look at your writing.

_____ Is it clear and neat?

_____ Can others read your handwriting?

WRITING PRACTICE TEST
Write your final composition here.

Tennessee Curriculum Framework English/Language Arts

WRITING: Grades 3–5

Content Standard: The student will develop the structural and creative skills necessary to produce written language that can be read and interpreted by various audiences.

Goal Statement: Writing is a lifelong, interactive process that is used to communicate with a variety of audiences and for a variety of purposes, adapting language conventions appropriately according to context. Writing is an act of discovery, a means of personal growth, and a tool for clarifying knowledge. To accomplish writing tasks more effectively, students need exposure to a variety of strategies, such as those included in the stages of the writing process, in order to approach writing systematically.

Learning Expectations	Practice Test Items	Assessment Options
• Write to acquire knowledge, clarify thinking, improve study skills, gain confidence, and promote lifelong communication.		S, T, PO, PR, PE, E, D, LJ, W
• Write frequently for a variety of purposes such as narration, description, and personal, creative expression.		S, T, PO, PR, PE, E, D, LJ, W
• Begin to identify and write for a variety of audiences.		S, T, PO, PR, PE, E, D, LJ, W
• Use elements of the writing process as appropriate to the writing task.		S, T, C, PE, D, LJ, W
• Practice a variety of prewriting activities to generate and organize ideas.		PO, PR, C, PE, E, D, LJ, W
• Use appropriate organizational strategies to develop writing, including main ideas and supporting details.		PO, PR, C, PE, D, LJ, W
• Demonstrate effective writing style by the use of vivid words, varied sentences, and appropriate transitions.		PO, PR, C, PE, D, LJ, W
• Begin to evaluate and revise writing to focus on purpose, organization, transition and audience.		PO, PR, C, PE, E, D, LJ, W
• Recognize and demonstrate appropriate use of standard English: usage, mechanics, spelling, and sentence structure.	7–9, 16–18, 24, 25, 36, 37, 40–42, 50–52, 59, 60	S, T, PO, PR, PE, E, D, LJ, W
• Begin to identify and use resources to revise and edit writing.		PO, PR, O, PE, E, D, LJ, W
• Continue to respond actively and imaginatively to literature.		S, T, PO, PR, O, PE, E, D, LJ, W
• Develop an understanding of and respect for multicultural and ethnic diversity in language.	1, 3	PO, PR, O, PE, E, D, LJ, W

Assessment Key

S	statewide test	**O**	observation
T	teacher-made tests	**PE**	performance
		E	exhibition
PO	portfolio	**D**	demonstration
PR	project	**LJ**	log/journal
C	checklist	**W**	writing

Tennessee Curriculum Framework
English/Language Arts

READING: Grades 3–5

Content Standard: The student will develop the reading skills necessary for word recognition, comprehension, interpretation, analysis, evaluation, and appreciation of the written text.

Goal Statement: Reading is a lifelong process which builds on language development. Students must apply a wide range of strategies to enhance the reading process. They improve their comprehension of printed information and gain knowledge of themselves as world citizens through varied experiences with literature. As students respond to texts individually and share in literary communities, they become critical readers and experience increased comprehension and personal satisfaction.

Learning Expectations	Practice Test Items	Assessment Options
Experience and develop an interest in literature which includes multicultural, gender, and ethnic diversity.	1–6	PO, PR, O, PE, E, D, LJ, W
Apply a variety of reading strategies.	1–60	S, T, PO, PR, O, PE, E, D
Extend reading vocabulary utilizing sight words, phonetic and structural analysis, and context.	1–60	S, T, PO, PR, C, O, PE, E, D
Improve comprehension by interpreting, analyzing, synthesizing, and evaluating written text.	1–6, 10–16, 19–22, 27–36, 43–50, 53–58	S, T, PO, PR, C, O, PE, E, D
Use comprehension strategies to enhance understanding, to make predictions, and to respond to literature.	1–6, 10, 11, 13–15, 19–22, 27–34, 43–49, 53–57	S, T, PR, O, PE, E, D, W
Read orally to develop fluency, expression, accuracy, and confidence.		T, C, O, PE, E, D
Read independently for a variety of purposes.	1–6, 10–16, 19–22, 27–36, 43–50, 53–58	S, T, PO, PR, C, O, PE, E, D
Utilize sources of information including technological tools.		T, PR, O, PE, E, D
Develop study skills to facilitate learning.		S, T, C, O, PE, D
Develop skills in making inferences and recognizing unstated assumptions.	5, 13, 23, 38–39, 45 49, 55–57	S, T, PR, O, E, D, LJ, W
Identify literary genres.		S, T, PR, PE, E, D, W
Identify and interpret figurative language.		S, T, PR, O, E, D, W

Assessment Key

S	statewide test	**O**	observation
T	teacher-made tests	**PE**	performance
		E	exhibition
PO	portfolio	**D**	demonstration
PR	project	**LJ**	log/journal
C	checklist	**W**	writing

© Scott Foresman 5

Tennessee Curriculum Framework English/Language Arts

VIEWING AND REPRESENTING: Grades 3–5

Content Standard: The student will use, read, and view media/technology and analyze content and concepts accurately.

Goal Statement: Visual communication is becoming an essential element of today's rapidly changing technological society, and students must be prepared for the demands they will face in the twenty-first century. Students must learn how to communicate effectively using visual media for specific purposes and audiences. Furthermore, as consumers, they must develop the skills to discern and evaluate the persuasive devices inherent in multimedia and technology. Educators must provide students with the necessary tools to function productively in tomorrow's world.

Learning Expectations	Assessment Options
• Use technological reference sources.	PO, PR, C, O, PE, E, D, LJ, W
• Use media to view, to read, to write, and to create.	T, PO, PR, O, PE, E, D, LJ, W
• Locate and organize information from print and non-print media.	PO, PR, O, PE, E, D, LJ, W
• Develop the use of the computer as a research and communication tool.	PR, O, PE, E, D, LJ, W
• Use multimedia to create and to display information.	PO, PR, O, PE, E, D, LJ, W

Assessment Key

S	statewide test	**O**	observation
T	teacher-made tests	**PE**	performance
		E	exhibition
PO	portfolio	**D**	demonstration
PR	project	**LJ**	log/journal
C	checklist	**W**	writing

Tennessee Curriculum Framework English/Language Arts

SPEAKING AND LISTENING: Grades 3–5

Content Standard: The student will express ideas clearly and effectively in a variety of oral contexts and apply active listening skills in the analysis and evaluation of spoken ideas.

Goal Statement: Throughout their lives, students will communicate through speaking and listening as informed individuals, as employees and co-workers, and as family and community members. When students explore the connections such as audience, speaker, purpose, and form, they become more versatile and confident in the choices they make as language users.

Learning Expectations	Assessment Options
• Increase confidence and poise in speaking.	PR, O, PE, E, D
• Use complete sentences in spoken language.	PR, O, PE, E, D
• Follow and give oral instructions.	S, T, PR, C, O, PE, E, D, LJ, W
• Demonstrate appropriate etiquette in speaking and listening situations.	T, PR, O, PE, E, D
• Speak and read using appropriate pronunciation, inflection, pauses, pitch, rate, and volume.	T, PR, O, PE, E, D
• Construct meaning from verbal and non-verbal cues.	S, T, PR, O, PE, E, D
• Use appropriate language structure in oral communication.	T, PR, O, PE, E, D
• Use a variety of activities to generate, develop, and organize ideas for oral communication.	T, PO, PR, C, O, PE, E, D
• Develop an outline, using notes and pertinent data, for an oral presentation.	PO, PR, C, O, PE, E, D, LJ, W
• Produce, present and/or perform original or published literary works.	T, PR, O, PE, E, D
• Participate in small and large group discussions by making relevant contributions.	PR, O, PE, E, D

Assessment Key

S	statewide test	**O**	observation
T	teacher-made tests	**PE**	performance
		E	exhibition
PO	portfolio	**D**	demonstration
PR	project	**LJ**	log/journal
C	checklist	**W**	writing

It was a sunny afternoon. I was in my doghouse. It was real peaceful except for one thing, Bullo, the mean nayberhood dog. I try harder to get away. He always gets me. Well anyways my owners are Ben, and ben's parents, Bill and Bernice. "I'm coming for you Rover, he yelled." I ran for my life to Ben's house. I forgot they've gone out! I started running toward the street. It was probaly rush hour because a lot of cars were on the street. I was lucky. Bullo got stuck in the traffick. I found Ben.

Amanda is smart, serious, and good. She was smart, she knew the bread was OK. She is serious when she solves the mystery. She was good, she tries to get back home by noon. Sherlock is hungary, nice, and smart. He was hungary when he wants a choclate thing. He is nice sometimes. He is smart when he solves the mystery. Amanda and Sherlock are more nice then lots of kids, but I wouldnt want to be freinds. They like to solve mysteries, I don't.

One day I was on the beach. I was swimming. I was practicing my strokes. Swimming at Diamond Beach in sunny July weather. All was going well until a shark decided to pop up and everybody run out of the Ocean. Ecept for my younger brother Bradley. He saw the shark near him. He waved madly. I had to save him. So I jump in the water strugled to get Bradley away from the shark and than I did. We swam back to shore. We never went to Diamond Beach again.

● I am alone at night. In a tent. All of a suden I heard a thumping sound coming from outside. I look outside to see what creture it is, but there was nothing there. All that I see. Is the dark night. I go back into my tent I take one last look around outside to

● see where I am and I get grabbed around the neck! Then I look around and realize that it was all a dream. I am still in my room. In bed. I realize that I am still in my pijamas and decide to go back to sleep.

Harriet Tubman was a slave, she didnt want to go to the South. But some mens were coming to take her to the south. She and her brother's runned away into the forest. I think they should just say they wont go to the south. The noises scared her brothers, they probably thought there was lots of big, feerce animals in that forest. But really only owls and frogs. They said their going back home. Harriet wanted to keep going, they wouldn't let her. Finully, she goes back to.

The food on page 75 looks nasty. And fake. I'll bet its been sitting their for an hour! The stuff in that picture on page 645 looks more good. Those strawberries look real. I would like to eat everything. Except for that round cokonut thing. I hate cokonut! The cupcake looked good. With the choclate frosting. You can bake this stuff for my freinds and I anytime.